DICTIONAI
BRITISH
VIOLIN AND BOW
MAKERS

By

DENNIS G. PLOWRIGHT

1ST EDITION

EXMOUTH

1994

Printed and bound by:-

BARTLETT PRINTING LTD.
Swan Yard, St. Thomas, Exeter

ISBN No. 0 9523081 0 X

Published by: -

DENNIS G. PLOWRIGHT
28 Raleigh Road
Exmouth, Devon
EX8 2SB

FOREWORD

It is a great pleasure to be asked by Dennis Plowright to write a few words to preface his "Dictionary of British Violin and Bow makers". Having known the author for many years I am well aware of his dedication to the subject over several decades.

I have been impressed by the compilation of this Dictionary which is thorough and professional. Many makers not listed elsewhere are included and in some cases the inaccuracies of previous treatises are corrected.

All in all this volume will be of immense value to its readers who will find within its pages an excellent source of reference.

David Shirt
Maryport, January 1994.

PREFACE

The last published reference work dealing with British violin makers was published so long ago as 1920: this book "British Violin Makers" by the Rev. W. Meredith Morris is long out of print.

The collection of material for my book was commenced nearly forty years ago and I have taken every opportunity which has come my way to add to my knowledge of past British makers: many of the names to be found within are recorded for the first time.

No work of this nature could be produced without reference to the standard works of previous authors and in my researches I have consulted the dictionaries prepared by Jalovec, Vannes, Sandys & Forster, Henley, Woodcock, Honeyman and Morris; also articles and 'snippets' of information from the 'Strad' and other journals as well as auction house catalogues principally issued by Puttick & Simpson, Phillip's, Sotheby's and Christie's. I would also like to acknowledge the help I have received from many dealers, collectors and musicians. A great deal of the information has resulted from my personal handling of instruments which I have owned or repaired, viewed at auction sales or been permitted to examine by their owners.

Hopefully there are not too many errors: it is too much to expect that there are none. I would be interested to hear of any facts which might be incorporated into a second edition or of any errors or omissions which might then be corrected.

Dennis G. Plowright
28 Raleigh Road, Exmouth.

ABRAHAM R.M. *Tewin*
Amateur maker c. 1940. He wrote a series of articles on violin making for the "Strad".

ABSAM Thomas *London, Wakefield & Leeds*
Worked c 1816 - 1850. Name sometimes spelt "Abson". His work shows certain German characteristics. His violins are on the Strad model but more highly built and the workmanship reasonably good. Violas small in body – 390mm; 'cellos also small 730mm. In one of the latter was written "Made by Gough & Absam, Cow Lane, Leeds": this was neatly made and varnished a yellow colour.

ACTON Charles *Manchester*
Worked c. 1880. Probably an amateur; very reasonable work.

ACTON, William John (1848-1931) *Woolwich & Forest Gate*
Worked at Forest Gate after 1898. He made all four instruments as well as viola da gambas and bows. His work is prolific but it is not highly finished generally and many of the violins are over the normal body length and have rather flat arching. The varnishing varies, at times it is of really good quality golden-brown in colour but some deep red varnishes have badly crazed. Mostly he used figured woods although his 'cellos are made from rather plain or slightly figured materials. M/S label "William John Acton/Maker/Forest Gate, London 1914".

ADAMS, Cathune *Garmouth*
Worked around 1775-1805. Passable work on the Amati style. Wood mostly plain or slightly figured, ink lines often replace the purfling, the scrolls not well carved and the varnish a pale yellow/brown.

ADAMS, Colquhoun *Garmouth*
It is presumed that he was the grandson of the former. His work is very much better but there seems to be little of it.

ADAMS, J.A. *Wellington*
This name was seen in a passably well made 'cello using plain materials covered with an orange brown varnish. The label undated but the period would be c. 1850. Label "J. Adams/Maker/Wellington Salop".

ADAMS, Henry Thomas (b. 1873) *Abbey Wood & Plumstead*
An amateur maker but his instruments show very good workmanship on the Strad model with slightly higher arching, strong edge work and covered with a fine oil varnish. The materials are good, well figured woods and fine to medium grained tables. Label "Made by H.T. Adams/No.12. Abbey Wood/Kent 1914". His output was not large.

ADDISON William *London*
Worked c. 1670.

ADIN Charles *Manchester*
His work is not very good. Label "Chas. Adin/1882/Manchester".

AIRETON Edmund (1727-1807) *London*
Thought to have been trained by P. Wamsley. His violins are on the Amati style, of good workmanship, neatly purfled and generally varnished a golden-brown. The tone is of good quality but not powerful. Violas very similar. His 'cellos are nice, generally small in body, fairly highly arched and with a flattish portion under the bridge; often ink lines replace the normal purfling. He made instruments for dealers e.g. C & S Thompson and Norris & Barnes and sometimes his name may be found written inside these on the upper treble side of the back.

AIRTH William (b. 1840) *Edinburgh*
Pupil of James Hardie (1). Worked at Edinburgh until 1881 when he emigrated to Australia.

ALEXANDER G.H. *Windsor*
Worked as an amateur c. 1890 with fair results.

ALEXANDER John (b. 1871) *Aberdeen*
Amateur maker whose output was not large. An example dated 1921 was well made but the deep red oil varnish had crazed badly. Label M/S "John Alexander/Aberdeen/1921". His name and date written on the top block.

ALEXANDER John *Birmingham*
Professional violinist. Worked at violin making with Thos. Simpson and J. Brierly of Birmingham. His work is good and well finished but his output was small. No. 17 dated 1953.

ALLAN James Campbell (b. 1923) *Balham & Hassocks*
Self taught amateur who received some help from E. Voigt. He worked on the Strad model, initially at Balham and, from 1960, at Hassocks, Sussex.

ALLAN James *Port Glasgow*
Amateur maker of average ability c. 1900.

ALLEN Hugh (b. 1894) *Abbey Wood*
An amateur who started making violins in 1921 following the Guarnerius style. His work is neat and nicely varnished.

ALLEN Samuel (b. 1858) *London*
Bowmaker. Worked for Hill & Sons for several years and on his own since 1891. A fine craftsman; some of his bows are beautifully mounted but frequently the sticks are very weak. He also made a few violins of good workmanship.

ALLEN Hugh

ALLEN W. 19th century *Bristol*

ALLEN W.J. b.1880 *Dorking*
An amateur maker.

ALLIN Joseph First quarter 20th century *London*

ALLKIN Edwin William b. 1887   *Nottingham*
Amateur maker who produced about 30 violins and violas of reasonable appearance and satisfactory tone. Varnish red or golden yellow often put on to give a worn look. No label but signed on inner back "Edwin Allkin/ 39 Ella Road/Nottingham/1921".

ALLWOOD Thomas   *Barnstaple*
Worked about 1860 and made violins on the Guarnerius pattern, but oversize, quite neatly. Branded ALLWOOD below the button.

ALLWOOD Thomas   *Glasgow*
The name of this maker was seen in a well made violin on the Guarnerius model varnished brown. The name inscribed on the inner back and branded below the button.

ALTON Robert b. 1881   *London, Leeds, St. Helens, Rock Ferry*
Not a prolific maker being very occupied with repairs. Better known for a book which he wrote on violin making and repairing which, however, gives a good deal of inaccurate advice.

ANDERSON A. Worked c. 1920-1930   *Edinburgh*

ANDERSON D.   *Glasgow*
Worked for G. Duncan c. 1900 and later on his own account. His work is not very good. Label "David Anderson/Maker/Glasgow".

ANDERSON Henry b. 1839   *Edinburgh*
Worked c. 1880 and made about 120 violins on a model akin to the Guarnerius. His work is quite good. Unlabelled but his name is written inside the back and sometimes stamped on with a punch.

ANDERSON John   *Aberdeen*
Pupil of M. Hardie. Worked in Aberdeen until his death. Prolific maker but very variable in the quality of his work: the best not the epitome of refinement yet the cheaper ones quite satisfactory. He varnished them with an oil varnish of an indeterminate brown colour. Label "Made by/John Anderson/Aberdeen".

ANDERSON John b. 1856   *Glasgow*
Violinist, teacher and maker who produced a large number of well made instruments using the Strad model. Printed label "Made by/John Anderson/Bon-Accord Violin Maker/Glasgow, 18- -".

ANDERSON William   *Gateshead on Tyne*
Label "Wm. Anderson Maker/No.66 Gateshead 1843.

ANDREWS Edward b. 1886   *Gt. Yarmouth*
A cabinet maker who took up violin making and produced about 30 violins and violas. These are quite well made but on the heavy side. He also made some bows which are appreciated. Label "Edward Andrews/Great Yarmouth/No. 24 1950".

ANGELL Frederick Stanley b. 1886   *Bristol*
An amateur maker who produced some excellent work making violins, violas
and 'cellos. Wood well figured, model after Stradivarius but broader, corners
long, nicely raised edges, all varnished with a good oil varnish generally golden-
brown in colour: this varnish he prepared himself and sold to other makers.
Label printed "Frederick S. Angell/Maker.Bristol/ 19..".

ANGELL Sydney 1883 - 1919   *London*
Worked for J. Chanot but also made about 70 violins and violas bearing his own
name; these are cleanly made on the Strad pattern and generally varnished red.

ANTROBUS Cyril b. 1883   *Wickham*
Commenced making in 1926 as an amateur. His model is an original one, the
edges too prominent and the whole conception heavy. They are nicely
varnished with a red or red/brown varnish.

ANYON Thomas   *Manchester*
An amateur maker who produced some instruments of fine workmanship, but
mostly over long in the body. Whilst his materials are satisfactory the maple is
generally fairly plain. Varnish an oil preparation. M/S label "Thomas Anyon/fecit
Manchester 1892".

ARCHER Charles 1904-1993   *Chelmsford*
Artist and violin maker. He spent a year in the Dolmetsch workshop and from
1947 to 1986 devoted his time to making and repairing violins and painting.

ARDERN Job 1826-1912   *Wilmslow*
He was a carpenter obsessed with making violins while selling them was of
secondary importance. At his death hundreds of instruments had accumulated
and these were bought by Hill's. The model is following Amati, fairly highly
arched, the body frequently over long, the edges rather prominent and the
corners heavy, soundholes long, all rather original but neatly done. They are
generally varnished shades of golden brown but occasionally one finds a
red/brown or red instrument. He seems to have made only violins. Some are
labelled with Hill's label giving his dates of birth and death others with his own
label "Job Ardern/Wilmslow/ No. 355. Cheshire 1899".

ARDETON   *Liverpool*
The name given by Rushworth & Dreaper to violins, violas and 'cellos made in
their own workshops (instruments labelled 'Apollo' are importations generally
from Markneukirchen). The Ardeton instruments are well made and in 1923
sold for £20 violins, £25 violas and £40 'cellos. They are made on the Strad
model generally although Amati and Guarnerius models were supplied. The
materials are excellent and they are oil varnished often in red. The red shades
of varnish have often begun to crackle. The 'cellos while nicely made of choice
materials are rather on the heavy side and the tone is hard to produce. Label
"The 'Ardeton' violin/Made throughout in the/workshops of Rushworth &
Dreaper/11-17 Islington-Liverpool/No. 270 Anno 1928".

ARMSTRONG Alexander   *Smethwick*
A pattern maker who, as an amateur, made over 100 well finished instruments
in the last quarter 19th century.

ARMSTRONG Matthew c. 1930   *Glasgow*

ARNOLD John   *Swansea*
Professional violinist who, as an amateur, made a few neatly constructed violins. He worked c. 1920.

ARNOT David 1831-1897   *Glasgow*
Initially an amateur maker he later turned to being a professional and worked from a shop in Stockwell Street. His early instruments are on the small side and rather highly arched but later ones were either on a Strad or Guarnerius pattern. The workmanship throughout is good and although the wood he used is sometimes plain his violins are attractive. The varnish he used is of good quality and in shades of brown. M/S label 'David Arnot/Glasgow 1887".

ASHLEY G.   *London*
Worked about 1760. His work is very ordinary and typical of the London 'trade' instrument of that time.

ASHTON John b. 1859   *Bury*
Self taught amateur who made only a few violins but these are neatly made and nicely varnished.

ASHTON Walter   *Colne*
Worked at 7 Keighley Road. Son of the above. Worked c. 1920-1935 and produced some neatly made instruments.

ASKEW John 1834-1895   *Stanhope*
A shoe maker who took up violin making and made a success of it. His instruments are on the Strad model using handsome woods and of fine workmanship the edges and corners very graceful and the scroll carving fine. Only in the varnishing have some of his instruments failed since some, especially those which are varnished deep red, have crazed badly.

ASKEY Samuel   *London*
A pupil of Morrison who worked from about 1780-1830. The quality of his work varies considerably. A good deal of it is not labelled since he worked for dealers. For a time he worked with G. Corsby.

ASPINALL James b. 1855   *Bolderstone*
An amateur maker whose output of violins and violas totalled about three dozen. His work is neat and covered with Whitelaw's varnish. Label "James Aspinall/Violin Maker & Repairer/ Bolderstone/nr. Sheffield".

ASTLEY -. Worked c. 1780   *London*

ASTOR -.   *London*
Worked c. 1790, his work has much in common with the trade type of violin then being made.

ATKINS James b. 1824   *Cork*
Proprietor of a music shop. He made a number of violins on the Strad model which are reported to be good both in workmanship and tone.

ATKINS John 1848-1919 *Sheffield*

An amateur maker who took up making violins late in life. He made about 20 instruments - violins and violas and one 'cello. The woodwork while quite neat has an amateurish look about it. Label "Made by/J. Atkins/No.7 - 1913". Sometimes branded J. ATKINS by the tailpin.

ATKINSON William 1851-1929 *Tottenham & Paglesham*

Made over 240 instruments, violins, violas and a few 'cellos. His work is finely finished and the materials he used always of the best. The model of his violins is original. He was particularly proud of his varnish but in this department he was sometimes unsuccessful since now some of his work is covered with a dry and crazed coating. His scrolls are very well carved and the chamfers picked out in black as are the rib joints, edges nicely raised, the corners left thicker than the edges which gives them rather a chunky look. Label "William Atkinson/in Tottenham 1892" and No. 84 added in ink on the top block.

AULDERO Tommaso Giacomo

Pseudonym used by J. Holder. Sometimes given as Tom°. Gia° Auldero/fecit Napoli anno 18 –"

AUSTINE, A. Worked c. 1890 *London*

BACHE, A.E. *Blackheath*

An amateur maker of no great ability who worked c. 1915.

BACON, T.W. *London*

He worked in Endell Street c. 1890. No. 27 was dated 1901.

BAILEY, James b. 1856 *Grimsby*

A self taught amateur maker who made violins, violas and 'cellos of adequate workmanship and satisfactory tone. Label "James Bailey/Violin Maker/76 Weelsby Street/Grimsby 1924"

BAILEY, Sydney b. 1890 *Woking*

An amateur maker c. 1925.

BAILEY, W. *London*

A bow maker who worked for Hill's and left them in 1940.

BAINES, –. *London*

A pupil of Matthew Furber and worked c. 1780: his violins are well made and nicely finished.

BAKER, Ernest James b. 1902 *London*

Was employed by Dykes and Sons. He produced a number of good violins on the Strad model.

BAKER, Francis *London*

He principally made six stringed viola da gambas working in St. Paul's Churchyard, but also made a few violins. c. 1700.

BAKER, John   *Oxford*
Possibly brother of the above. He mainly made viols but a few highly arched violins are known. c. 1700.

BAKER, William   *Oxford*
Probably the father of the two preceding. His name is to be seen in a small 'cello 712mm body length dated 1672.

BAKER, William   *Brighton*
Worked c. 1820-1840 and made some good violins as well as some of little merit sometimes having grotesque carved heads in place of the customary scrolls. He is best known for having made some excellent double basses.

BALDWIN, S.W.L.   *Balham, London*
An amateur maker c. 1920 whose work is good. He used a manuscript label and branded his name S. BALDWIN inside the back.

BALDWIN, Thomas   *Birmingham*
An amateur maker of small ability.

BALMFORTH, Leonard Geoffrey 1909-1967   *Leeds*
Made only a few instruments since he was occupied mainly with repairs and running his well known shop in Merrion Street.

BALMFORTH, Leonard Percy 1881-1936   *Leeds*
Taught by Paul Bailly. Not a prolific maker but his violins on the Strad model are very well made and nicely varnished a deep red/orange colour.

BANKS Benjamin I 1727-1795   *Salisbury*
New light has been shed on this family as the result of research by Mr. Albert W. Cooper. Banks was apprenticed to W. Huttoft (d. 1747), Musical Instrument maker of New Sarum in 1741 for a term of seven years. Huttoft worked in Catherine Street and when he died Banks, who had not completed his apprenticeship, took over the workshop. Banks' earliest known violin dates from 1755. His violins are modelled after N. Amati, A & H Amati and a few after Stradivarius. The work is good, the edges neatly worked and the corners delicate. The scrolls are less satisfactory appearing in some instances flattened. Usually the varnish is a dark red, or shades of red, applied satisfactorily except sometimes to the tables where frequently it has sunk into the soft grain thus making this darker than the hard grain. The violas are of small size ranging from 380mm to, exceptionally, 400mm - most commonly 390mm. The 'cellos are the best of his instruments; in common with Old English work they are of small proportions mostly 735mm body length but he also made a few on a longer rather ugly pattern 745mm body length: best are the Amati style 'cellos 735 body with the stop set at 387mm. The tone of these is not large but of remarkably even and pure quality. He made no basses. Some instruments are known stamped Longman & Broderip and ascribed to Banks. In his own work various labels are used and his work is often stamped in several places either BB or B. Banks.

BANKS, Benjamin 11 1754-1820   *Salisbury, London, Liverpool*
Son of the above and worked with his father until 1780 when he moved to London. Unfortunately he did not do very well there probably because his work was certainly not very good. He later moved to Liverpool where he died in 1820.

BANKS James 1756-1831   *Salisbury & Liverpool*
Son of Benjamin 1 and worked with his father until the latter's death. He then entered into a partnership with his brother Henry until 1811 when they both went to Liverpool working first in Church Street and later in Ward Street. There James continued to make instruments (Henry made no violins so far as is known). The work may be labelled James & Henry Banks but it is the work of James alone in most cases very like his father's. Some of his instruments are branded BB or B. BANKS which leads to confusion, this may have been done by the trade long after the instruments were made to 'cash in' on the greater reputation of Benjamin Banks 1. Sometimes a brand J. & H BANKS/LIVERPOOL is used below the button particularly on 'cellos. Another label is "Banks/Ward Street/Liverpool/1820".

BANKS James   *London*
A little known maker but one who had much ability. His working period was a decade either side of the turn of the century. A fine viola 405 mm body length made from handsome woods, well made, 'cello type heel to pegbox and varnished red/brown was labelled "James Banks/Maker/London 1898/No. 31". Instrument No. 48, a violin, was dated 1900.

BARCLAY Andrew 1856-1918   *Dundee*
An amateur maker who made a few violins and 'cellos of fair merit and reputedly good tone.

BARKER, George b. 1870   *Chesterfield*
He worked on the Strad model and produced some good violins during the first quarter of the 20th century.

BARLOW Arthur b. 1860   *Braunton*
A chemist who made about 30 violins as well as a few violas and 'cellos. His models were Stradivarius and Guarnerius but not close copies in any way, the work is neat using good materials and the results successful. The varnish, an oil one, is generally shades of red. The name and date written on the inside of the back.

BARNES - .   *Waterford*
c. 1890. Known only by an attractive violin bearing his name.

BARNES A.   *London*
Bowmaker who worked for Hill's whom he left in 1939.

BARNES Frederick c. 1890   *Accrington*

BARNES G.A.   *Manchester*

BARNES George W. c. 1900   *Belfast*

BARNES Robert   *London*
Apprenticed to Thomas Smith. Went into partnership in 1765 with Norris a fellow apprentice, as dealers. Instruments bearing the name Norris & Barnes or his name (Robert Barnes/Violin Maker/Windmill Street, Haymarket) are the work of others either in their employment or as outworkers: thus the quality of the instruments is very variable.

BARR Robert   *Belfast*
Worked c. 1910, well made instruments using good materials and nicely finished but the plates are too thick which stifles the tone.

BARRETT John   *London*
Worked c. 1710-1740. While some of his work is not very good there are many neatly made instruments to his credit: previous notices have unjustly denigrated his efforts. The violins are small, rather high in modelling, wood nicely figured (generally small figured sycamore) and neatly worked, well purfled (although some have only ink lines in place of the purfling) and covered with a good golden brown varnish. His 'cellos are inclined to be thin in the plates and the tone small; the materials of good quality, the outline rather straight top and bottom, body length 735mm and the varnish either similar to the violins or red/brown. Various labels from the Harp & Crown in Coventry Street near Piccadilly.

BARRETT Kershaw   *Haworth & Oxenhope*
A mining engineer who, between about 1900 and 1935 made a number of good violins, violas and 'cellos. The violins are on the Strad model using well figured woods, neatly made and finished off with an excellent oil varnish. The violas are large in size - 425mm - and similar to the violins. The 'cellos are a little small at 730mm body length and well made. The varnish is a fine orange/brown or red/brown, very transparent and nicely polished. His instruments are a credit to amateur making.

BARRY F.D. 1870-1926   *London*
A professional musician and pupil of Frank Howard. He made a large number of violins on standard classical models and these are of good workmanship and nicely varnished. He also made a few bows.

BARTON George   d. circa 1810   *London*
Worked between about 1770 and 1810 principally making instruments for the trade. His signed work is not often seen and it is not particularly good. Label "George Barton/Maker/London 1806".

BARTON John   *London*
Brother of George and the better craftsman of the two. He also worked for the trade about the same period as George but his personal work is more frequently encountered than that of his brother. The violins are on the Amati model using well figured wood for the backs etc. and good spruce for the tables. The work is neat, nicely purfled, well finished off and varnished generally golden brown. Inside it may be a different story the backs being smoothed but the tables just left roughly cut by the gouge; it does not seem to matter to the tone however which is good. He made also less well finished instruments of plain wood, ink lines for purfling, hasty work and poor varnish.

Violas are small but usually nice: I have not seen any 'cellos. He worked as an outworker for C & S Thompson and his name is sometimes found signed inside their instruments.

BARTON J.E. b. 1846 *Llanelli*
Worked c. 1870-1930 and made a large quantity of instruments of generally satisfactory workmanship on the Strad model and a shade on the heavy side.

BASTON Victor *Southall & Beaconsfield*
An amateur maker who worked c. 1945 to 1965. His work is of average quality. He made several Tertis model violas which design was very popular at that time.

BATCHELOR H.C. *Luton*

BATHO W.J. c. 1890 *London*
Violin and double bass maker.

BAXTER A.C. *Middlesex*
Amateur maker who produced some nice violins and violas c. 1935.

BAXTER M.L. *Glasgow*
Worked c. 1860; very reasonable amateur type work.

BEAMISH John *London*
Worked as an assistant to W. Glenister and made a few violins during the first quarter 20th century.

BEARD John 1919-1992 *Ealing & Sarratt*
A professional violinist who had some tuition in violin making from W. J. Piercy. His work is on various models and being inconsistent it may be said that each production was slightly different from that which had preceded it. Whilst his instruments were not highly finished, indeed some were rather rough, many of them sound very well.

BEARD, R. *Aylsham*
An amateur maker and repairer c. 1960; his instruments are not very well finished.

BECKETT John 19th century *Faversham*

BEE F.C. circa 1920 *Shiremoor*

BELL A. *Camborne*
Worked c. 1920 and produced a number of violins and 'cellos which are nicely made.

BELL John M *Birkenhead*
Maybe an amateur maker: he worked in the period 1910-1920.

BELLINGHAM T.J. 1853-1927 *Leeds*
A self taught amateur maker who achieved a good reputation during his lifetime. He made about 100 violins and violas which are nicely made, well varnished and have an attractive appearance: as regards the tone of his instruments this was praised by many authorities. At his death Boosey & Hawkes bought the remainder of his instruments. Label "T.J. Bellingham/fecit Leeds/No. 11 September 1904".

BELMAN James c. 1890

BELOE W.L. 1819-1897
Made violins and violas using principally the Strad model also a few 'cellos. He was a prolific maker and his work is quite good and covered with a varnish of his own composition. Label M/S "Made by/W.L. Beloe/Coldstream/ 1889".

BENSON James *Stanhope*

BERNARD J. b. 1865 *Cupar*
Amateur maker who made about a dozen violins during the years 1922 to 1932, they are quite nicely made generally from plain hardwood and varnished red/brown or golden/brown.

BERRY P. b. 1879 *Kirkaldy*
An amateur maker who produced a few very well made violins made from the best materials and oil varnished a deep golden brown.

BERRY, R.W. d. 1916 *Chesterfield*
An amateur maker who worked c. 1900. He used the Strad model for his violins and these are quite well made.

BERTRAM W.A. b.1801 *Eddleston*
A prolific but mediocre worker.

BERTRAM W. *Stobo Castle*
Amateur maker.

BETTS, Edward d.1817 *London*
Pupil of Richard Duke. Most of his violins are on the Amati model but he occasionally copied other makers. His work is first class with fine modelling, purfling, soundholes and scroll carving. The varnish is also good, this is in shades of brown mostly dark. His Amati style instruments have a tone of sweetness and quality but not powerful. His instruments are very infrequently labelled.

BETTS John Edward 1755-1823 *London*
Pupil of Richard Duke. He made a few instruments on the Amati model in good fashion but speedily found that there was more and easier money to be had by dealing and having instruments bearing his name made for him by others. Thus he employed workmen of ability such as Carter, Tobin, Panormo etc. and for cheaper instruments turned to the trade makers of the period. The best instruments, still mainly of the Amati pattern, are generally fine using good materials and nicely varnished. The 'cellos bearing his name or stamp are

excellent, often larger than the 'Old English' size then prevalent and flatter than the violins and violas. One sees many anonymous instruments, particularly 'cellos often with ink lines instead of purfling, offered by dealers as 'School of Betts'; there seldom seems to be any justification for linking his name with such productions. Some 'cello bows are seen stamped BETTS, these were probably made for him by John Dodd.

BEVERIDGE William 1820-1893   *Tough*
Became a professional maker but not wholly occupied in violin making and repairing: nevertheless he managed to produce a large number of instruments, violins and violas, which are well made and finished. Some are labelled others branded "BEVERIDGE TOUGH" inside the back.

BIDDULPH H. 1866-1949   *Aberystwyth & Wandsworth*
A pupil of Frank Howard. His work is excellent, the violins generally on the pattern of Guarnerius. He also made violas and 'cellos: his work deserves to be more appreciated than it is.

BIRD C.A.E.   *London*

BIRCH Thomas   *Hereford*
Worked between about 1840-1860; his work is quite good.

BIRD Richmond Henry b.1869   *Wolverhampton & Liverpool*
Worked at Wolverhampton until 1914 when he left to take charge of the violin workshop of Rushworth & Dreaper in Liverpool. His personally labelled work numbers some 55 instruments on classical models which are very well made, but he also made some (but by no means all) of the 'Ardeton' instruments bearing his employer's name. His work is excellent. Label "Richmond H.Bird/81 Raleigh Rd., No.45 1912".

BIRNBAUM, A.J.   *London*
The name of this maker was seen in a very well made violin No. 81 dated 1924.

BISHOP Edgar 1904-1943   *London*
A bowmaker who worked for Hill's.

BLACK G.G.   *Basildon*
c. 1950 Amateur work of little merit.

BLACK M.   *London*
An amateur maker c. 1960 who made a number of violins and violas of very reasonable workmanship.

BLACK James   *Dundee*
c. 1840 Neat work on the Strad pattern.

BLACKBURN J.H.   *Colne*
An amateur maker c. 1920.

BLACKMORE Richard 1869-1939   *East Dulwich*
He was an amateur maker employed by the Admiralty as a model maker and
thus a skilled woodworker; he also played the violin. He made over twenty
violins on the Strad model and of good workmanship, well cut scrolls and
soundholes, carefully inlaid purfling and excellent edgework. Only in the
varnish was he less than successful since that on the fronts is very blotchy due,
no doubt, to putting the coloured varnish direct on to the bare wood. M/S label
"R. Blackmore/East Dulwich/16 London 1922".

BLACKWOOD W.   *Galashields*
An amateur maker of above average ability. He used a large pattern Strad model
362mm body length. Label M/S "William Blackwood Galashields/1900".

BLAIR William 1793-1884   *Dunkeld*
A pupil of Peter Hardie of Dunkeld. Originally a carpenter he made a great
number of violins but they are not very good.

BLAIR John   *Edinburgh*
Worked from 1790-1820 towards the close of that period with Matthew Hardie.
His violins on the Strad pattern are usually made from handsome wood and
varnished a pale brownish shade. They are unlabelled but his name is sometimes
written inside the table and JB stamped on the table under the fingerboard.

BLAKEMORE G.   *Walsall*
An amateur maker c. 1950 who made some violins and a few violas on the
Tertis pattern. No. 10 dated 1948.

BLIGHT R.   *Exeter*
Nicely made violins Amati style but not too highly arched, golden brown
varnish. Name branded below the button. He worked circa 1830.

BOGG M.   *Duggleby*
Rather poor quality work. Label "M.Bogg/Maker/Duggleby/1858".

BOLTON Arthur   *Walsall*
Worked at 34 Ryecroft Place. In the period 1950-60 he used regularly to
advertise his "£10 handmade violins oil varnished" in the 'Strad'.

BLYTH Williamson 1821-1897   *Edinburgh*
A prolific maker credited with having made over 2,000 violins. Few of his
instruments are much good. Whilst the outside work could be quite neat
he used unsuitable models (some violins as long in the body as 372mm)
and worked the plates very thin so that the sound they make is feeble.

BONE, Philip J.   *Luton*
Made some violins around the turn of the century (No.18 dated 1889 nicely
made but the varnish very opaque). He was head of a music firm in Luton,
which firm was still in existence in 1970.

BOND William   *Totnes*
He worked c. 1820.

BONN Edwin J. 1861-1927   *Brading*
Originally a chemist. He became interested in violin making and, after tuition, gave up chemistry and became a professional maker and repairer. His violins are on a modified Strad model and neatly made; he also made violas and 'cellos. In addition he sold various items of his manufacture for string players such as a four footed bridge, varnish cleaner, "Bonn's Patent Retinine for Violin Pegs", resin etc. Label "J. Edwin Bonn/Brading/Isle of Wight".

BOOTH Charles   *Burnley*
Worked c. 1890; average class of work.

BOOTH Joseph   *Manchester*
Average work, woods plain or little figured, ink lines for purfling, golden varnish. Label "Joseph Booth fecit/March 28th 1879".

BOOTH William I 1780-1853   *Leeds*
Worked c 1810-1850. Work rather ordinary but not at all bad. Dark golden brown varnish nicely applied. Label "William Booth Maker/Leeds 1834".

BOOTH William II 1816-1856   *Leeds*
Son of the above and a better maker than his father in fact some of his violins are very nice indeed. The best are on the Strad model and covered with a very superior golden brown varnish: others are rather big in the body - 354mm length. He also made violas and 'cellos and some of the latter are rather good.

BOREHAM Arthur   *London*
He worked c. 1920 and produced some excellent violins.

BORLAND Hugh
A little known maker and his place of work is not known. A good violin dated 1903 was well made, slightly big, and varnished a yellow colour.

BOTHWELL William   *Aberdeen*
Period c. 1870-1885. Made about 100 poorly made instruments which are not labelled.

BOUETTE Maurice Kenneth 1922-1992   *Northwood & Newark*
Received instruction from William Luff at an evening class. Later took up making repairing and teaching making at evening classes as a living. His own work is not prolific. He set up the Newark School of Violin Making and was its first Head.

BOULLANGIER Charles 1823-1888   *London*
Came to London to work for Withers in 1849 having previously worked for Vuillaume and Gand & Bernadel in Paris. He opened his own shop in Frith Street in 1856. His work is first class in all respects but some instruments in the 1870's were supplied to him 'in the white' from Mirecourt and these he finished off: working on his own he was not particularly prolific. He employed A.R. Meynell and J.J.T. Wilson. After his death the firm continued until 1913.

BOURKE Thomas b. 1867   *Edmonton*
A cabinet maker who made his first violin in 1896; his violins are rather large in the body, often of one piece of wood for the backs, well made and generally varnished shades of red on a yellow ground. Label "T.Bourke/Edmonton, 1917".

BOWEN Thomas A.E. b.1909   *Clapham, London*
An amateur maker; small production.

BOWER Andrew   *Grangemouth*
Worked c. 1900 and made some large bodied violins of adequate workmanship.

BOWLER Arthur b.1867   *London*
A joiner originally who went to work for J.A. Chanot for five years from 1895. He
set up in business for himself in 1899 at 18 Milner Square, Islington. He made
several instruments while with Chanot. Most of his personally labelled violins are
based on the 'Messie' Strad: his work is excellent using fine woods, the edges
clean and sharp, corners likewise, fine modelling and covered with a good oil
varnish generally a deep orange/brown. His prices in 1899 were Violins £8
upwards, 'cellos £12 upwards. Label "Arthur Bowler/London fecit 19– (AB)".

BOWMAN Alfred John b.1861   *Peckham*
After some years undertaking repair work he made his first violin in 1918. He
was taught by William Robinson and his work is quite satisfactory but he made
few instruments.

BOYER J.A.   *Aberchirder*
A minister of the Church who made about 30 instruments in the Strad style and
of average workmanship.

BOYLE W.F. b.1860   *Enniskerry*
An amateur maker who made a large number of instruments of excellent
workmanship on the Strad pattern and then spoiled them by badly applying a
very poor home made varnish.

BRADDYL H.S. b.1910   *London*
'Axed' from the Navy he opened a shop in the Royal College of Music dealing in and
repairing violins etc. He made only a few instruments including two 'cellos; these are
well made using good materials. The varnish he used was devised by a friend E. Crump
and consisted of proprietory artists oil varnishes blended with colouring materials: one
of these being asphaltum rendered the varnish very erratic in its behaviour.

BRADLEY E.J. 1901-1992   *Shirley*
He made relatively few instruments and these are of rather amateurish work
and covered with a slightly opaque varnish. He also undertook repairs and sold
violin making wood.

BRATTER Leonard   *London*
An amateur maker who was taught by W. Luff c. 1960; he made relatively few
instruments.

BRAY F.   *Middlesbrough*
An amateur maker.

BRAYSHAW James   *Lancaster*
He worked c. 1850 making violins and 'cellos. He used no label but wrote his
name etc. on the inside of the back.

BRAUND F.T. 1890-1991   *Colchester*
A pupil of F.W. Channon. He made his first instrument in 1927 and his last, aged 92, in 1982. The model is based on that of Stradivarius as modified by his teacher, the wood generally handsomely figured and the excellent workmanship nicely set off by a superior varnish mostly red/brown in shade. The tone of his instruments is praised by many.

BRECKENBRIDGE John 1790-1840   *Glasgow*
An amateur maker and probably self taught: though his output is not large his Amati style violins are finely made of excellent materials, well varnished a light brown colour and highly regarded tonally. Label "John Breckinbridge/Maker/Parkhead 1834".

BRIERLEY Joseph   *Birmingham*
Worked in Birmingham c. 1900-1930. His instruments are excellent using handsome wood treated to capable workmanship and the whole covered with a splendid varnish red/brown or golden/orange in colour. M/S label "Joseph Brierley/Birmingham fecit Anno 1922".

BRIGGS James William b. 1855   *Wakefield, Leeds, Glasgow*
Pupil of Tarr in Manchester. First worked at Wakefield (No. 26 dated 1888), then for a short while in Leeds and finally in Glasgow. His best violins are on the Guarnerius model but longer in the body, excellent woods and very fine work. He made some 'cellos and these are on the heavy side with strong edges, the tone hard to produce. Nice shades of varnish but this is inclined to be chippy.

BRISCOE D. 19th century   *Channel Islands*

BROAD J.M.   *Almondsbury*

BROCK J.   *Carlingcott, Bath*
An amateur maker who made a few violins and double basses c. 1930.

BRODIE Robert   *Maryport*
He was an amateur maker who made a number of violins of good but slightly heavy workmanship on a model not unlike that of Degani. He used very good materials and his varnish, a deep red laid on a golden ground, while inclined to be soft is of excellent quality. The tone of his violins is powerful yet has quality.

BROOKFIELD Edward & Son   *Southport*
Worked between about 1870-1914 making good violins and bows.

BROOMFIELD George b.1880   *Runningburn*
An amateur who made about 40 good violins using both Strad and Guarnerius as models.

BROUGHTON Leonard W.   *Southampton*
A little known amateur maker who left a large number of instruments at his death.

BROWN A.   *London*
A bowmaker with Hill's; he left their employment in 1958

.BROWN Alexander   *Glasgow*
He worked about 1860 and completed about 70 instruments on the Strad
model well made and nicely finished. M/S label "Alex Brown/Maker/Glasgow
1858".

BROWN Antony   *Clerkenwell*
Worked c. 1850-1875 when he left for Australia. He assisted Panormo and his
violins are neatly made but nothing much tonally. His instruments are
sometimes labelled "Antonio Bruno".

BROWN Charles F. b.1893   *Blackburn & Wakefield*
His instruments are neatly made on the Stradivarius and Amati models.

BROWN J.   *Huddersfield*
He worked at Huddersfield for over 50 years and made a large number of rather
ordinary looking instruments - violins, violas, 'cellos and double bassc, - whic'1
are not improved by the dull brown varnish which he used. Of his large output
the cellos and basses are the best works. His work is generally labelled with a
wordy printed label but some are just stamped J. BROWN on the back.

BROWN J.   *Wakefield*
Worked there about 1855 but his work is not good.

BROWN James I 17 9-1834   *London*
Pupil of Kennedy. Established his workshop in Spitalfields. The violins are
rather on the small side, the corners long and 'hooky' the scroll well carved but
the eyes over long, bottom ribs in one piece, workmanship not bad and often
the varnish is really nice in a rich red colour. Occasionally he applied geometric
designs in purfling on the back.

BROWN James II 1786-1860   *London*
Pupil of his father and his violins are very similar to those of his instructor. He
made a large number of bows and those for the 'cello are particularly liked.

BROWN James III b.1815   *Dundee*
Son and Pupil of James II; he made only a few instruments and these nothing
much before giving up the business in 1838.

BROWN James S.   *Newcastle*
Probably an amateur maker who worked c. 1925.

BROWN R.   *Kintore, Aberdeen*
His label was seen in a well made violin on the Guarnerius pattern made from
good materials and covered with a golden/orange varnish. Label M/S
"R.Brown/Kintore Aberdeen 1932"

BROWNE John   *London*
Worked c. 1735. His early instruments small and tubby but later ones more on
Amati lines and of better workmanship altogether: they are mostly 352mm body
length and have one piece backs which although generally plainish are sometimes
very handsomely figured. The varnish is golden/brown or orange/brown in colour.
Sometimes labelled but often the name is written on the inner back.

BROWNE J. & Sons   *Grimsby*
Their name is seen in instruments but these have a continental look about
them. One however, dated 1890, may have been made either by a workman in
their employ or by an outworker. "J. Brown & Sons/Musical Instrument
Makers/35 Victoria Street, Grimsby".

BRUCE Arthur   *Belfast*
Worked c. 1900 and made several very fine violins covered with a good varnish.

BRUCE A.B. b.1866   *Glasgow*
Made over 60 instruments - violins, violas and 'cellos - of excellent
workmanship and carefully finished and varnished.

BRUCE James Grant b.1896   *Newport, Fife*
His output though small is of good quality. His violins follow the Guarnerius
model the first one being made in 1916.

BRUCE James W. c.1890   *Glasgow*

BRUNSKILL J. d.1901   *Berwick & Newcastle*
He worked at Berwick from 1880 to 1893 and at Newcastle thereafter until his
death. His violins are on the Strad pattern and the selection of materials and
workmanship excellent in every respect. Label "James Brunskill/Maker &
Dealer/175 Westgate Road/Newcastle-on-Tyne 1891".

BRUTON James c.1850   *Thornbury*

BRYANT Percival Wilfred 1902-1980   *London & Ovingdean*
Bowmaker. He worked for many years for Geo. Withers & Sons, later on his
own in London moving to Sussex in 1939. His bows are very highly regarded.

BUCHANAN David c.1940-1970   *Eynsham*
An amateur maker who made a few violins, violas and 'cellos of fair merit and
reputedly good tone.

BUCKMAN George Hatton 1845-1920   *Dover*
A self taught amateur. His violins are often large in body - 362mm - but he did
make some on more conventional Strad lines, for example a violin dated 1902
having a fine one piece back and being a handsome instrument in the Strad
style. Sometimes the varnish lets him down as some otherwise good
instruments are spoiled by now being covered with a dry and crazed surface
inimical to good tone. For the period in which he worked his violas are on the
large side. He made altogether about 60 instruments.

BULTITUDE A.R. 1908-1990   *London & Hawkchurch*
Bowmaker. Apprenticed to and worked for Hill's becoming Head of their
Bowmaking Department. He left Hill's to work independently in 1961 at
Hawkchurch. His personally stamped bows are often on the heavy side and the
sticks strong: frequently the frogs have Tudor roses inset in the sides.

BURLING Alfred James b.1870   *Islington, London*
He made about 40 instruments from his workshop in Theberton Street, Islington and was very busy as a repairer. The violins are chiefly on the Guarnerius model, nicely made and well finished. He worked at least until 1928. Label "A. J. Burling/London 1928".

BURNETT James   *Edinburgh*
He worked, probably as an amateur, circa 1925 and made some quite satisfactory instruments.

BUTCHER James   *London*
Worked at Templars Bar c. 1780 and produced some neatly made violins.

BUXTON James   *Bristol*
Worked at Bristol c. 1830 but not very effectively.

BYROM John   *Liverpool*
He was working at Liverpool c. 1902 from the evidence of a well made violin on the Strad pattern of good materials and varnished red/brown. Almost certainly related to George Byrom.

BYROM George 1870-1928   *Liverpool*
His instruments are not numerous but they are very good: he was well known for excellent repair work.

BYROM H.
Bowmaker. Stamped H. BYROM.

BYRON H.   *Oxford*
Worked c. 1800 and produced the Amati style violin popular at that time very satisfactorily.

BYWATER Henry   *Bristol*
His violins made circa 1800 are of small proportions and on the Amati model using nicely figured wood and varnished golden/brown. His violins are seldom seen. Label "Made by/Henry Bywater in Bristol".

CAHUSAC Thomas d.1798   *London*
A certain degree of mystery surrounds the instruments bearing this name; were they made by him or by others? The style and quality is variable but for the most part they are not well made, generally ink lines substitute for purfling, thin in the plates and covered with a dark varnish, often the bass bar has been fashioned from the wood of the table. This all points to the instruments having been made to order by various second class workman of London who made for the trade. It is said that there are some better class instruments on the Amati pattern using good materials treated to fine workmanship; this may be the case but it does not preclude the possibility that they were made by better workmen. His son, also Thomas, married Ann Banks daughter of Benjamin I in 1780 but there was no working connection between the families. Various labels e.g. "CaHuSac/London/1788".

CAIRNS Peter b.1846 *Edinburgh*
He worked at 18 Durham Rd., Portobello on a modified Guarnerius model. His work is heavy with strongly beaded edges, well formed but large corners etc. all suggestive of the work of a well trained joiner or cabinet maker since the workmanship is well executed. The varnish is generally a golden brown. Frequently used birds eye maple for the backs and ribs. A few made with the table larger than the back thus the ribs set at an angle. No label but inscribed inside the back "Peter Cairns/18 Durham Road/Portobello/Edinburgh".

CAKIN Francis c.1800 *Edinburgh*

CALOW Thomas 1868-1905 *Nottingham*
Son and pupil of William Calow. Mainly worked on repairs with his father but made a few instruments varnished brown with his name written inside the back.

CALOW Thomas *Tansley*
Grandfather of William. He made a few highly built violins and violas.

CALOW Francis William 1884-1952 *Nottingham*
Son of William and his pupil. He is the principal maker of the family but even so not very prolific. He worked at 16a Broad Marsh, Nottingham and made his first violin in 1922 on the Strad model, the edges very strongly raised, long corners, nicely figured wood, good workmanship and the whole varnished a deep orange/brown: this he sold for £12.10. He made a few nice 'cellos with similar characteristics. Instruments often stamped CALOW under the button and by the endpin. Label "Calow/Nottingham No.1 1922".

CALOW William 1847-1910 *Nottingham*
Made violins and 'cellos but is best known for his double basses of which he made about twenty. He also specialised in dealing in basses from his shop at 8 Sussex Street.

CANNON F.C. *Canterbury*
He was a pupil of Frank Howard and his instruments are well made: a viola 397mm body had a broad grained front and red/brown varnish. It bore a manuscript label "Frederick Charles Cannon/Maker/Canterbury 1931".

CANNON James b.1855 *Dumfries*
An amateur maker who produced above average work on the Strad model covered with a rather chippy varnish. Label M/S "J. Cannon/Dumfries/1888".

CARPENTER S. *Glasgow*
Probably an amateur maker; a violin dated 1892 was well made on the Guarnerius pattern.

CARR John 1839-1918 *Falkirk*
Learned to make violins from J. Thompson and R. Harvie of Berwick. He made over seventy instruments of all types following the Strad model. These are well made from handsome materials and nicely varnished in, generally, red/brown shades. Sometimes branded CARR on the back sometimes labelled e.g. "John Carr/Maker/Falkirk 1897".

CARR Richard   d.1922   *Gateshead on Tyne*
He completed about 20 violins which are well made, have a golden varnish which he made himself, and have a pleasant tone.

CARROLL James   *Salford and Manchester*
A prolific maker assisted by his son John. Their instruments are modelled on those of the classical masters. Their workshop was at 103 Great Jackson Street, Hulme. Label (printed) James Carroll, maker/Manchester, anno 18 —".

CARSWELL William   *Birkenhead*
An amateur maker c. 1915 whose work is of little merit.

CARTER John   *London*
Worked c. 1780. He undertook much work for Betts therefore not much is to be seen bearing his individual label. He worked on the Amati pattern using generally wood of small flame with good workmanship and golden brown varnish. His instruments are responsive in tone but of no great power. Sometimes he built instruments which have only 'ink line purfling' and plainish woods probably a cheaper class of violin. His violas are small. The 'cellos are nice instruments, quite highly arched and having a very pleasant quality of sound. Label "J. Carter/Violin, Tenor and Bass maker/Wych Street, Drury Lane/London 1785".

CARTER John   *St. Helier, Jersey*
Worked c. 1865.

CARTER William   *London*
Known only by a handsome and well made violin bearing his manuscript label dated 1932, 355mm body length, Strad pattern, orange brown varnish.

CARTER-WALKER, Thomas (1908-1982)   *Chessington*
He was a professional 'cellist and friend of George Wulme-Hudson who gave him advice on violin making and repairs. He made a few violins all on the Joseph Guarnerius model and two violas between the years 1943 and 1975. He was an expert repairer particularly of double basses. Some instruments are labelled "Joseph Nankivell - Surrey". Nankivell is a family name.

CARTWRIGHT W.J. 1836-1919   *Yeadon, Leeds*
Pupil of Joseph Fox and later worked with H. Pickard of Leeds. The numbers on his labels seem to indicate that he made over 1,000 instruments but they seem to be scarce. His work is rather rough considering his training but the varnish is of very nice quality.

CAVILL A.   *London*
Worked c. 1910, probably an amateur. His work is quite good.

CAYFORD, Frederick   *London*
Worked c. 1880, good work.

CHANNON F.W. 1862-1946   *Plymouth, London, Weybridge*
A joiner and cabinet maker who turned to violin making. He first worked at 40 Cumberland Road, Devonport until 1912 when he moved to Wells Street,

London: later he worked at Weybridge. He made about 50 violins, a few violas and one 'cello; these are of varying quality, some are allegedly copies of famous instruments but the violins are frequently over long in the body (as much as 363mm) and broad as well. Others are more standard in size. In some the length of the corners is pronounced and the edges protruding more than usual giving a distinctly amateurish look. The workmanship is however good so that these features were intentional rather than the result of inability. The varnish is a very good one, mostly in golden brown shades, and well applied: tonally his instruments have given satisfaction.

CHANOT A.E. b.1890   *London*
Son and pupil of F.W. Chanot and worked at 29 Rathbone Place. He was a very good repairer who made relatively few new instruments but these are of first class workmanship the violins being on Strad and Guarnerius models and varnished deep orange brown. His violas are of a small/medium size (395mm). Some of his instruments have tables made from rather broad grained wood.

CHANOT Frederick William 1857-1911   *London*
Son of George III and pupil of Georges II in Paris. Returning to London he established himself in Berners Street in 1874: here he made, sold and repaired violins and also ran a music publishing business ('Edition Chanot). He made about 90 instruments which have a typically 'French' look about them, these vary in quality. Later he moved from Berners Street to Soho Street and instrument No. 68 dated 1893 is ticketed as from 'Covent Garden'.

CHANOT Georges III 1830-1893   *London*
Pupil of his father Georges II in Paris. He came to London in 1851 to work for Maucotel remaining with him until 1857 when he opened his own workshop in Wardour Street. He made a large number of instruments of fine workmanship, the best violins are on the Guarnerius model but slightly larger as is the French style. He also made bows but these are not always entirely satisfactory, they are stamped CHANOT.

CHANOT Georges Adolphe 1855-1923   *Manchester*
A prolific maker with the model of the instrument generally stated on the label. Some of the copies are rather eccentric in dimensions and style but the workmanship is always good; occasionally the work is decidedly heavy and chunky. The materials invariably nicely figured and the varnish also good. His 'cellos are excellent but sometimes very big. His instruments are numbered and dated but it seems not always in strict sequential order.

CHANOT John Alfred b. 1904   *London*
Son of Joseph Antony and assisted his father until the latter's death after which he worked from his home in Tulse Hill.

CHANOT Joseph Anthony 1865-1936   *London*
Son and pupil of Georges III and took over his shop on his father's death. He made a large number of violins and a few violas which are excellent in every respect; his best violins are on the pattern of Joseph Guarnerius, frequently the backs are in one piece. A fine repairer and esteemed as a dealer and expert. He made a few bows and these are stamped J.A. CHANOT. Label "Made by/Joseph Anthony Chanot/No. 160 London 1913".

CHANOT William Arthur b.1899   *London*
Son of Joseph Anthony and his assistant; he made a few violins but was mainly engaged on repair work. After 1936 he worked on his own at Winterbrook Road, SE 24.

CHAPPELL Lewis Thomas b.1870   *Forest Gate*
He was taught by George Pyne. He made few instruments but these are of excellent workmanship. He learned bow making from James Tubbs and turned out many splendid bows in the same style as his master generally unstamped: no doubt by now they bear the more illustrious name of his master. He was an instructor in bow making and violin restoration at the British Violin Maker's Guild.

CHASSERY Leon   *Birmingham*
Known only by a splendid violin 362mm body labelled "Leon Chassery/15 Constitution Hill/Birmingham", undated but the period around 1920: very well made, excellent purfling and corners, slab back, fine head, golden red varnish. Possibly a Frenchman who lived and worked here.

CHRISTIE James b.1857   *Dundee*
Very clean work using a large pattern Stradivarius model; later instruments favour the Guarnerius pattern. Early instruments rather heavily built but this later corrected to some degree. Varnish a soft oil type generally red or shades of red in colour. Printed label "James Christie/Violin Maker/Dundee" – the date added in ink.

CHRISTIE John William 1778-1859   *Kinkardine on Forth*
Made many instruments of reasonably good workmanship on a large Strad pattern, they are not very well varnished however. Nevertheless the tone of his instruments is good.

CHURCHWARD T.   *Dittisham*
He worked there between about 1800 and 1838 and made about 50 violins of quite reasonable workmanship, a few violas and at least one 'cello the latter of 750mm body length varnished golden brown and labelled "Made by T. Churchward/Dittisham 1838".

CLARE Harry 1884-1960   *Merthyr Tydfil and Newcastle*
He was taught by J.E. Harris. His work is well made and finished but rather heavy in conception using good materials and varnished with an oil varnish of his own making (thus he marketed for other makers). Sometimes the varnish has developed a slight crackle.

CLARK Edwin   *Sidmouth*
An amateur maker who worked as a tailor in Mill Street about 1900-1920. He made some reasonably well finished violins and repaired those of local players: he also made some bows and rehaired others using hair from the tails of the dray horses of Vallance's Sidmouth Brewery. He was known locally as 'Wonderful Clark'.

CLARK James   *London*
He worked c. 1800. Matthew Furber was his teacher and he made quite satisfactory instruments like others of the period and covered then with a good varnish. Label "James Clark/Maker/Turnmill Street/Clerkenwell, London 1781".

CLARK William   *Exeter*
First quarter 19th century. His violins are reasonably well made on the Amati model of faintly figured wood and not purfled; varnish golden brown.

CLOUGH George b.1881   *Blackburn*
He worked from about 1908 to 1930 and was probably self taught. His violins are well made on a rather individual model which is 360mm body length. His deep red or deep red/brown varnish is fine. Label "1928/George Clough/Violin Maker/Blackburn".

COAD Albert b.1884   *Camborne, Redruth & Penzance*
Workmanship and materials are good but some features such as the over prominent edges with a deep scoop by the purfling are overdone and spoil the otherwise good effect. He made principally violins, the early ones often over long (e.g. 'Mozart' dated 1912 at 362mm) but later ones of more normal measurements. His varnish is good and applied in several shades of which a deep red is the best. He made some violas and 'cellos but not many of these. Label "A. Coad/Camborne/Cornwall/ 'Mozart'. Fecit 1912".

COATES R.   *Belfast*
Worked c. 1920, an amateur maker of little talent.

COCKER Lawrence b.1908   *Derby*
A prolific maker, amateur at first then professional; he mainly made violins but also some violas (Tertis model generally) and a few 'cellos. The workmanship and choice of materials coupled with a Strad model carefully followed gave him good results but the varnish on some of the early instruments has crackled quite badly. He made a large number of bows using split cane for the sticks, the head and handle being made from pernambuco wood joined to the cane by a vee graft.

CODD F.   *Devonport*
He was an amateur maker who produced very reasonable work using good materials. The label in one read "Made for Miss F. Wooland by her friend F. Codd of Devonport 1894".

COCKCROFT William   *Rochdale*
He worked near Rochdale about 1850. His work is quite good on a long bodied model of 362mm. Materials of good quality. Well flamed hardwood and nicely varnished golden brown. M/S label "Willm. Cockcroft/near Rochdale/March 18th 1851", also stamped W. COCKCROFT below the button.

COCKMAN F.C.   *London*
An amateur who c. 1920 made a number of eccentric violins to test certain theories on tone.

COCHRANE James   *Dundee*
He made over 300 instruments during the period about 1880-1925. These are made on various models and the work is very satisfactory.

COCHRANE William   *Dundee*
Maybe related to the former maker.

COLE James *Manchester*
A pupil of William Tarr and worked c. 1845-1890. His work is unequal. The best are on the Guarnerius model and these are accurately made and of good workmanship and finish but others are not at all good and obviously made quickly for a cheap sale. Some are labelled e.g. "James Cole/fecit Manchester/1884" while others are merely stamped J.COLE below the button (sometimes both labelled and stamped as in a well made violin 360mm body dated 1884).

COLLARD & DAVIS *London*
Their label "Collard & Davis, Makers/No.7 Fish Street Hill, London" proclaims them to be makers but most probably instruments bearing their name were made for them by journeymen makers working for the trade. Thus these instruments vary in quality but some are very nice.

COLLINGWOOD F.W. *London*
An amateur maker who produced a number of good violins on a large Guarnerius model. The workmanship is very satisfactory and the varnish a fine deep red/brown.

COLLINGWOOD Joseph *London*
He worked c. 1735-1779. He made a large number of violins on the Stainer and Amati pattern as well as a few on other models, best are the Amati style instruments where good wood is treated to excellent workmanship and nicely varnished generally golden brown shades. Few instruments are labelled and his work is therefore less recognised than it should be; it is conjectured that some of it is now giving pleasure to players in the guise of Italian work.

COLLINS William Henry b.1860 *London*
An amateur maker self taught. He made some excellent violins on the Strad model and a few following Guarnerius. Working period 1890-1915.

COLLISON Alfred *London*
An amateur maker who was a winner when presenting a violin dated 1905 to the Industrial Exhibition Newington Green: this was a nicely made and well finished instrument covered with a soft orange brown varnish.

COLTMAN M. *London*
A bow maker with Hill's who left the firm in 1981.

COLVILLE David *Cupar*
Worked c. 1845-1885, for part of this time he lived in New Zealand and some instruments were made there. Previously a cabinet maker his workmanship is good. His violins are mostly modelled on the Strad pattern and the backs and ribs well figured, the plates are rather thick but in all other respects his instruments are well made. They are unlabelled but his name is written inside the back – "David Colville/1861".

COLVIN Gavin 1841-1910 *Sunderland*
He made his violins on an oversized Strad model with satisfactory workmanship and tonal results, the edges are rather prominent and the corners nicely finished. Printed label "Gavin Colvin/Maker/Sunderland/1893".

CONKERTON E.R.   *Newark*
An amateur maker who worked c. 1920.

CONNOR Anthony c.1920   *Newcastle*

CONWAY William   *London*
He worked c. 1740. His violins are small and rather highly arched, varnish
golden brown. Label "William Conway/London 1746".

COOK A. Mid 19th century   *Ipswich*

COOPER A.E. b.1857   *Ulverstone*
A minister of the Church who made some quite good violins and 'cellos as an
amateur, they are on Stradivarian lines.

COOPER Hugh William b.1848   *Glasgow*
He made over 100 instruments mainly on the Strad pattern but some on the
Guarnerius model. His instruments are attractive, nicely figured backs, good
edgework and corners, scroll well carved and finished off with an oil varnish
(sometimes the red varnishes have crackled) of deep red, red/brown or orange
brown shades. Label "Hugh W.Cooper/ Maker 75 Dundas Street, Glasgow/No.
73 1902".

COPLEY A.   *London*
First a case maker then a bowmaker who worked for Hill's. Died 1976.

COPLEY N.   *Middlesbrough*
Known only by a fairly well made violin labelled "N. Copley/Maker/
Middlesbrough/1903". Somewhat Stradivarian in model, small figured wood to
back and ribs, golden varnish.

CORSBY George   *London*
He worked between about 1790 and 1930. His instruments are pretty ordinary
but not badly made. The violins are generally made from wood of small figure,
probably English sycamore, the corners often over long and 'hooky', the body
on the small side: sometimes slab cut sycamore is used with the back in one
piece. The 'cellos are similar often using slab cut wood for the backs; they are
rather longer, 750mm is typical, than English 'cellos of this period: generally
ink lines take the place of purfling. The varnish is thin in quality and in shades
or red/brown and golden/brown. Label "George Corsby/Maker/Princes Street,
Leicester Square/London". Sometimes stamped CORSBY below the button.

COTTRILL J. b.1879   *Torquay*
An amateur maker who left some very nicely made instruments; they are made
on individual patterns, the wood and workmanship is excellent and they are
generally covered with a rich red oil varnish. Between the years c. 1923 and
1936 he made some twenty violins, they are 'numbered' by the letters of the
Greek alphabet.

CRAB Vincent   *London*
Known only by a 'cello labelled in manuscript "Vincent Crab/London/'78".

CRAIG Thomas   *Aberdeen*
Violins are often seen labelled "Thomas Craig, Aberdeen". These were not
made by him but are mainly German instruments, occasionally French, which
he labelled, numbered and dated. They are generally quite good for their class.

COX, Henry   *Swaythling*
An amateur maker who worked c. 1938; his work is fairly good.

COX N. c.1920   *London*

CRAIG John b.1860   *Edinburgh*
A joiner by trade who made a large number of good violins on the Strad model
slightly heavy in style and nicely oil varnished. Printed label "John
Craig/Maker/Edinburgh/A.D. 1899".

COX Henry   *Dublin*
He worked c. 1840 but not very well.

CRAMMOND Charles   *Aberdeen*
He worked from about 1800 to 1845 and was a prolific maker. The model of
his violins is fairly high and generally the wood is worked too thin for the tone
to be satisfactory. The varnish is a nondescript shade of brown on wood of
small or no figure, the table wood mostly fine grained. Looking on the back the
pegbox barely tapers to that the first turn of the scroll is partly hidden, the
throat open, short upright soundholes with large bottom circles. Body length
often on the large side. His 'cellos are small often 730mm body with ink lines in
place of purfling and like the violins made from wood practically devoid of
figure and covered with a brown varnish. His instruments are sometimes
labelled with a printed label "Chas.Crammond/Maker/Aberdeen 1823",
sometimes with a label in manuscript and often unlabelled but with
CRAMMOND/ABERDEEN stamped on the back below the button.

CRASKE George 1795-1888   *London, Leeds, Sheffield,*
                                                  Birmingham and Salford
The most prolific maker working single handed known in this country and,
possibly, in all countries. He is credited with having made over 2,500
instruments in his own name to which must be added the ones he made for
Forster, Dodd and other dealers. He was taught by William Forster. Many of his
violins are 'copies' of Italian masters yet they are not copies in the strict sense
of the word often being dimensionally inaccurate. Bearing in mind the speed of
production it is astonishing how well finished the majority of them are and in
addition good wood (often very handsomely figured maple for the backs and
ribs) has been used and generally covered with a fine varnish, rich in colour
and of good texture. Of course there are exceptions, and furthermore such
speed of working leaves no time for regulation of the tone and here his
instruments fall down since the tone is 'woody' and unresponsive - this due to
his practice of leaving the wood of the tables far too thick. The models used
vary, perhaps the Guarnerius model is the one which produced the best results;
some of the violins are over long in the body. The violas vary from about
395mm to 405mm and some of these have a very flat arching sometimes as
little as 13mm for the back and the tone is poor. 'Cellos represent his best
work, yet here again some have very flat arching and the tone suffers in

consequence. He also made double basses. Present day prices are far above the true worth of the majority of his instruments when they are judged on tonal standards yet one must give recognition to such industry and capable craftsmanship.

CRINDLE J.M. *Glasgow*
An amateur maker who worked c. 1875 and turned out some quite reasonable violins.

CROFT W.H. *Birmingham*
A professional violinist who worked also at violin making in the last quarter of the 19th century. He made all four bowed stringed instruments and his work is quite good.

CROMBIE Thomas *West Wemyss*
He worked c. 1815.

CROSBY G.R. c.1900 *Dewsbury*

CROOK E. *Redhill*
An amateur maker who completed only a few instruments on the Strad model. M/S label "E.Crook/Redhill,Surrey/1963".

CROSS H.C. *London*
He was taught by Timothy Toomey of Enfield and, as an amateur maker completed 11 violins, 4 violas and 1 tenor; the work is of average ability.

CROSS Nathaniel *London*
He worked from about 1700-1750. It is not known from whom he received his training but his early work is not too good, highly arched, blunt corners and a deep channel inside the edge, all a sort of Stainer model. Later work is more tasteful, the arching reduced but still rather high, improved soundholes and excellent nicely rounded edges yet still the moat inside the edges remains. The varnish is thin in texture and light brown or golden brown in colour. He made some violas about 405mm body length and these are excellent, also 'cellos which are on the small side - 730mm - with deep ribs, fine edgework, nicely purfled and having a flattish area underneath the bridge: they are very sonorous.

CROSTON J. *Leigh*
An amateur maker c. 1920.

CROWTHER John *London*
He worked c. 1750-1800. His labelled work is seldom seen since he spent most of his time working for others especially John Kennedy. Those violins that are labelled are small in size, of medium arching and rather wide at the top. The work is quite good and the backs generally nicely figured which is brought out by the red/brown varnish. His son, also John, worked with him.

CUMMING Andrew b.1848 *Portpatrick*
A self taught amateur maker who worked c. 1890 and completed about 50 violins of rather poor workmanship and finish.

CUNNINGHAM P. *Cambusbarron*
An amateur maker who worked during the first quarter 20th century and made some very satisfactory violins.

CURRIE A.W. c.1950 *Liverpool*

CUTHBERT James *Hownam*

CUTHBERT Robert *London*
Worked in the 3rd quarter 17th century at the White Horse in Russell Street. He made his violins from pretty wood on a small model with arching distinctly flatter than was in vogue at that time. They are varnished red/brown shades.

CUTTS W.B. *Hull*
Known by a 'cello dated 1900 bearing a printed label. This was made from good materials and, up to a point, well made but heavy and amateurish looking with some essential dimensions e.g. neck length and stop incorrect: all pointing to the work of a non-professional.

CUTTER Edwin b.1866 *East Compton*
A wheelwright who made a large number of quite well made violins but the model he used is not a good one and frequently the woods he used were not suitable for the purpose.

DALGARNO Thomas *Aberdeen*
He worked during the third quarter of the 19th century and made about 20 violins, a few 'cellos and a double bass. His work is neat and carefully done but the plates seem to be rather thin and the tone is weak. He used a handwritten label "Thomas Dalgarno/Aberdeen 1866".

DALTON B. *Leeds*

DARBEY George 1849-1925 *Bristol*
He worked in Perry Row, Bristol between about 1880 and 1920. He was trained as a wood carver and cabinet maker so that the mechanical side of making and repairing caused him no difficulty. His work is very good, most of his violins are on the Strad model and are made from finely figured wood treated to first class craftsmanship. He was a capable violinist and this no doubt assisted him in the production of violins which sound so well. The varnish too is of good quality, generally red/brown or orange brown, it has plenty of 'fire' in its appearance. He also made a large number of bows which play well but are not exactly beautiful in the hatched shaped heads: some of his bows are mounted in gold and ebony with engraved mounts. His output is not known since he did not number his labels and his instruments are seldom seen.

DARNEY Alexander *Kingsborn*
Probably an amateur maker who worked c. 1890. His work is quite neat and nicely varnished with a golden brown oil varnish.

DAVIDSON Kay *Huntley*
He worked c. 1870 but not very well.

DAVIDSON Peter 1834-1901 *Forres*
An amateur maker who left a number of instruments of very fair workmanship, most of the violins are on a model approaching that of Stradivarius but occasionally he used other models. He made his own varnish which is generally thin in texture and red in colour. He is better known for a book on violin making first published in 1871 which ran to four editions; like many on the subject the information contained therein has to be interpreted with care.

DAVIDSON, William 1827-1902 *Edinburgh*
He made a few violins and violas as an amateur maker circa 1880 and these are quite well made, the back wood faintly figured and the oil varnish red or red/brown in colour and rather thickly applied. Label "William Davidson/Edinburgh 1888".

DAVIES T. *Birmingham*
He was an amateur maker circa 1880. His violins and violas are quite well made, the wood faintly figured and the varnish red/brown. His instruments are labelled (No. 9 dated 1880) and branded T.DAVIES/BIRMINGHAM below the button.

DAVIS A.W.E. b.1901 *London*
An amateur maker second quarter 20th century.

DAVIS Richard 1775-1836 *London*
He was apprenticed to and worked for Norris and Barnes. He made few violins and these of not very good quality but he took over the Norris & Barnes establishment and achieved a reputation as a dealer who employed some good workmen.

DAVY William *Bolton*
He made violins and violas and worked at Bolton prior to 1914.

DAWES Jesse b.1904 *Longhope*
He worked on a modified Strad model very neatly and varnished his violins with a good oil varnish. Label "Made by/J. Dawes, Violin Maker/Longhope, Glos./No.*** A.D.19**".

DAY John 1830-1905 *London*
A professional violinist who made a large number of instruments as an amateur. Most of the violins he made are on the Guarnerius model but not correctly so since some are square on either side of the button and the sides of the top bouts are rather straight. The Guarnerius style soundholes have their length exaggerated and are set so that the bridge platform is narrow - a serious defect for good tone. All of the work is well executed and the woods selected for good appearance, the grain of the table is generally treated to make it stand out.

DAY W.S. (Senior) 1862-1943 *Liverpool, London, Plymouth*
An amateur maker whose work is dated from various places to which he was posted as a Customs House official. His work is very good mostly on a modified Strad outline but occasionally using the Guarnerius pattern. A typical violin dated 1923 from Liverpool had a finely figured one piece back, long corners,

nicely rounded edges, cleanly cut soundholes, strongly grained front and a good golden brown varnish just beginning to craze slightly. A descendant of the family said that the basis of the varnish was amber and for this old pipe stems were collected. His son (also William Samuel 1887-1958) opened a music shop in Plymouth in 1919 which closed in 1935 and after his retirement from the Custom's service W.S. Day Senior worked there: the shop was noted for excellent repairs. The son made only a few violins but a good number of excellent bows.

DEARLOVE Joseph Anthony   *Leeds*
Son of Mark William and his successor. He made few instruments and these are very ordinary. Branded on the back J.DEARLOVE/LEEDS.

DEARLOVE, Mark   *Leeds*
He worked from about 1810-1850 and made a quantity of quite nice instruments as well as some that are distinctly ordinary. The violins are flattish, the better ones of nicely figured wood and covered with a good golden brown varnish. They may be labelled or branded or both. The 'cellos are rather larger than the usual old English style of the period and the better ones are very nice but there are some seen with his stamp which are of poor workmanship and materials possibly made by others for him for a quick sale. He employed various workmen including Absam, Fryer and Gough. From his labels he worked at Boar Lane and later at No. 18 Bridge Street.

DEARLOVE Mark William   *Leeds*
He worked from about 1836-1876 first at 27 Black Swan Yard, Vicar Lane, then at 172 North Street and finally in Merrion Street. He is the best maker of the family and some of his Stradivarius style violins are very attractive. His 'cellos are on the small side, generally very nice and varnished red/brown.

DEAS John   *London*
He worked mid 19th century. His work is quite neat. He used no label but wrote his name etc. inside the back.

DEIGHTON J.R. First quarter 20th century   *Newcastle*

DELANY John   *Dublin*
A cabinet maker by training. He worked c.1795-1810. His work is variable in quality but his best violins are of small pattern, plainish wood, the soundholes short and rather open, the edgework and corners nicely done with a sort of groove from which the arching rises. Sometimes ink lines replace the proper purfling. The varnish of quite good quality generally light brown or golden brown.

DENNIS Jesse 1795-1860   *London*
He was apprenticed to John Crowther and later worked for Matthew Furber. After this he established himself at 16 Ewehurst Street, Walworth. His instruments leave a good deal to be desired considering his training; they are seldom seen and perhaps he was not a prolific maker. Label "Made by Jesse Dennis/16 Ewehurst Street, Walworth/London 1859"

DEVIS William   *London*
A watchmaker and amateur violin maker who worked about 1750-1765. His instruments are quite attractive and varnished a deep red/brown.

DEVONEY Frank 1854-after 1920   *Perth & Blackpool*
His instruments are rather variable in quality and on a somewhat peculiar
pattern added to which he had theories regarding tone production which
resulted in his violins being very heavy through excessive thickness of the
plates. Later in life he worked in America and abandoned his theories
producing some good violins reasonably well made and varnished with a
particularly fine varnish.

DEWARS William   *Brechin*
The workmanship of his violins is of a reasonably high standard using Strad and
Guarnerius models, they are made rather heavy around the edges and the plates
are left thick yet the tone is very fine. Later he emigrated to America and
worked in Minneapolis. Label Wm.Dewars/Maker/Brechin.Jan 12. 1902".

DICKENSON Edward   *London*
Worked about 1750-1790 at the 'Harp and Crown' in the Strand. His violins are
highly arched, thin in wood and poor in tone.

DICKESON John   *London & Cambridge*
His name is sometimes spelt 'DICKSON' on his labels. His violins are attractive
using pretty wood and varnished golden brown. His 'cellos are on the small
side about 725mm body length, they too are nicely made and finished and the
tone of them is of good quality and very suitable for chamber music. His
working period was from about 1750 to 1790.

DICKIE Matthew   *Rotherham*
He worked c. 1900. His violins are made on the Strad pattern and the
workmanship is very satisfactory. The golden brown varnish which he used has
a tendency to craze. Possibly he was the brother of William Dickie.

DICKIE Robert   *Stirling*
An amateur maker who produced several violins of average merit during the
period about 1915-1925.

DICKIE William   *Wentworth*
He worked from about 1880 to 1900. His violins are modelled mostly on the
Strad pattern but other models are seen, the workmanship is good as is the
golden red oil varnish with which they are covered.

DICKSON George   *Edinburgh*
He worked during the first quarter of the 20th century and was a Doctor of
medicine who made a few good violins but is better remembered for his amber
oil violin varnish: this was very slow to dry but popular in its day.

DIXON Alfred Thomas   *Dover & Folkestone*
He was a professional violinist with a large teaching practice. He became
interested in violin making about the turn of the century and, working until
about 1935, made a number of quite well fashioned violins.

DOBBS Harry   *Sutton Coldfield & Peopleton*
He worked as an amateur maker from about 1960 until his death in 1978. He
achieved good results and made a fair number of all three instruments using

good materials and with very satisfactory workmanship. (No. 98 dated 1972). Later examples were made from partly finished materials obtained from Germany. Some instruments were given fanciful Italian names e.g. Gasparo Rovelli, and these are stamped DOBBS on the top block.

DODD Edward 1705-1810 *London*
It is not known from whom he learned bow making. His early work follows the pattern of the day in England where the style of bow making lagged behind the improvements introduced in France, but over his long life this imbalance was redressed. Most of his work is unstamped or bears the name of the dealers for whom he made the bow.

DODD John 1752-1810 *London*
Bowmaker. He made thousands of bows of varying quality, the best being very fine indeed. The violin bows are short by today's standards and this prevents them ranking with the finest bows ever made. Probably his best bows are for the 'cello, these are often heavy and some made quite crudely for cheap sale often with an 'open' frog, but even these play well and many have been remounted with modern style frogs. His bows are stamped DODD in large letters on the stick and frog. Some bows are most exquisitely mounted with gold and gems. Many bows are seen stamped DODD on the stick and frog and underneath the DODD on the frog is the word 'Regd' in small letters: these were not made by Dodd but are German bows of very fine quality some made by Albert Nurnberger. They dated from about 1890-1910.

DODD Thomas I *London*
Third son of Edward Dodd, he worked from about 1776-1823. First a bowmaker but soon stopped this trade and opened a violin shop in New Street, Covent Garden later moving to St. Martin's Lane. He made a few instruments himself but employed other good makers chiefly John Lott and Bernhard Fendt to make them for him. He claimed (as many have done since) to have perfected a 'Cremona' varnish. All four instruments were made but maybe he produced more 'cellos than others since they are more frequently seen.The work is variable depending on the skill of the particular maker but the best is very good. Notwithstanding his claims for the varnish it has often worn very badly.

DODD Thomas II *London*
Son of the above; his work is rarely seen since he died very young.

DODD S.H.
Nothing is known of this maker other than a good violin bearing the enigmatic label "S.H. Dodd/Maker 1923". Another on a large Strad pattern was undated but numbered No. 95.

DODDS Edward 1817-1896 *Edinburgh*
He made about 300 instruments in Charlotte Place and like his more famous near namesake Thomas Dodd also had discovered the true 'Cremona' varnish. The workmanship of his violins is first rate and the scrolls particularly well carved with a large diameter eye and beautifully undercut. The prized varnish is however a let down as it is thickly applied, a pleasant red brown colour, yet soft and chippy.

DOOLEY James W. b.1910 *Dover & Glasgow*
Commenced making violins in 1926 and completed during the following 30 years a number of good instruments.

DOLLARD -. *Dublin*
Worked, not very well, circa 1840.

DONOVAN L.A. *Enfield, London*
He worked circa 1920 making violins and 'cellos and very nicely too.

DORANT William *London*
He worked from about 1800 to 1826 at 63 Winfield Street, Brick Lane. His work is very ordinary.

DOYLES J.J.H. b.1882 *Sunderland*
An amateur maker who commenced making in 1943. He made 10 violins, 6 violas and 1 'cello of quite acceptable workmanship.

DRYBURGH-SMITH E. *Sutton Coldfield*
His label was seen in a well made violin 355mm body length dated 1942 and covered with a good red/brown varnish.

DUCKWORTH Frank 1895-1981 *Blackburn*
He was an amateur maker and completed about a dozen carefully made violins and one viola at 66 Brantfell Road, Blackburn. The violins are on the Strad model, he used good materials, varnished them nicely and they sounded well.

DUFF William 1810-1882 *Dunkeld*
A gardener who produced a large number of rather crudely made and highly arched violins generally with ink lines instead of purfling, varnished with poor varnish of a yellowish colour.

DUGHLEY John c.1760 *Leicester*

DUKE Richard I *London*
He worked between about 1750 and 1780. His violins are many and modelled after Stradivarius, Stainer and Amati, best are the last named. His work is however very variable, the best is very good indeed. His reputation is to some extent damaged by the large number of trade violins stamped with his name - German Duke's - and often of poor quality bearing no resemblance to Duke's work. He frequently used nearly figureless wood and, even if figured, the rather thick red brown varnish tends to hide the flame; sometimes the varnish is a golden yellow colour. He made a good many violas often with one piece backs but also many which are small (typically 378mm body and 238mm across the bottom bouts) and with deep ribs, these do not sound well. He also made tenors of 455 mm body length. The few 'cellos he made are longer than the usual old English 'cellos of the same period but the plates are too thin and the modelling too high for satisfactory tone. He used various labels and often branded DUKE LONDON (sometimes only DUKE) below the button. Forgeries so stamped nearly always omit the LONDON.

DUKE Richard II   *London*
Son and pupil of the preceding but not such a good workman. He worked from about 1768 to 1790. He used the same stamp as his father and seldom labelled his violins. Labels "Duke Junr/London1771" and "Duke Jnr/Maker/Gloucer St.,Queen Square/London 1763".

DUNCAN George b.1855   *Glasgow*
He took over Walter Plain's shop in Brunswick St. in 1875 but later worked at 16 Queen St. His violins are well finished and generally follow a Guarnerius style, they are made from good materials and oil varnished, often a deep orange/brown. He emigrated to Canada in 1892. Label "George Duncan/fecit/Glasgow 1891" He won Gold Medals in London (1885) and Glasgow (1886 and 1887).

DUNCAN James b.1871   *Cluny*
Well made instruments on Guarnerius pattern. His first instrument - a 'cello - was dated 1898 and No. 27 dated 1910.

DUNCAN James b.1873   *Dunfermline & Kirkaldy*
He worked from about 1895 to 1950 and was a cabinet maker by training. His instruments are well made and satisfactory.

DUNCAN Robert   *Aberdeen*
He worked from about 1740 to 1780. His violins are highly arched, not purfled, the scroll rather small, soundholes short and set straight, not badly made from plain or small figured woods and varnished a yellow colour. The tone is small. Printed label "Robert Duncan/Maker/Aberdeen 17**".

DUNCAN William   *Gateside, Beith*
He worked in the first quarter 20th century, probably an amateur maker judging by the evidence of a Strad model violin dated 1912.

DUNLOP Alexander   *Broxburn*
He worked from about 1880-1900 and made some good violins on the Strad pattern. The backs are well figured and the fronts broad grained. The tone excellent. Varnish orange/brown. Label "Alexr. Dunlop/Maker 1883".

DUNTHORNE John   *East Bergholt*
Known only by a tolerably well made 'cello labelled "John Dunthorne/fecit East Bergholt Suffolk/May 16th 1798". Plain woods, ink lines in place of purfling, red/brown varnish.

DYER A.E. 1879-1972   *Exeter*
An amateur maker who completed several fairly well made violins but some are too large in the body.

DYKER George   *Forres*
An amateur maker who made about 50 instruments which show highly talented work using good materials and covering them with a fine oil varnish generally orange brown. The tone of these is excellent. Label "Made by/George Dyker.1920 Forres".

DYKES George Langton 1884-1922 *Leeds & London*
Pupil of Paul Bailly in Leeds. He made many instruments of fine workmanship but most of his time was spent in the family business supervising the work of the restoration department.

EADIE John *Glasgow*
He worked there about 1880 and made some quite satisfactory violins.

EADIE William *Milton Balgonie*
He worked c. 1950 and in his small brochure "Hidden Violin Secrets" claimed to be a maker although I have seen none of his work. The book is largely rubbish, the theory being based on the use of a bass bar very much deeper than usual.

EARL David J. d. 1984 *London & Greenford*
After serving an apprenticeship with Hill's he worked for them as a bow-maker until 1980 when he left to work for himself. His bows are very well made every part being fashioned with precision: in some frogs the sides are embellished with an Earl's crown.

EASTBURN W. c.1900 *Halifax*

EDGAR James *Kilmarnock*
An amateur maker c. 1900 whose work is very good.

EISENMANN H. *London*
He worked between about 1875 and 1890. His work is very satisfactory. His violins often have whole backs and are varnished with a dark red glossy varnish. The 'cellos are rather on the heavy side. Label "H.Eisenmann/Violin and Violin cello Maker/London".

ELLIOTT William *Hawick*
He worked from about 1885 to 1920 and made over 100 instruments of excellent workmanship and tone on the Strad model. The backs etc. are of prettily figured wood and his instruments covered with a soft red/brown oil varnish. Label "William Elliott/Hawick 1914" printed with a decorative border.

EMPSALL John K. *Ben Rhydding*
An amateur and dilletante maker. He was obsessed with the theory that fine tone stemmed from the varnish with which an instrument was covered and he formulated various varnishes which he tried out on violins and violas made for him 'in the white' (quite a few of these were made by Langonet in Hill's workshop). His varnishes vary a good deal but some of the instruments bearing his label are first rate. Later he made violins himself with some success. Label handwritten on parchment "John K. Empsall/Ben-Rhydding 1906" and numbered LXXI on the corner of the ticket.

ERVINE Robert *Belfast*
He worked from about 1890-1925 and made about 200 instruments of good workmanship the violins being modelled after Stradivarius and made from choice woods oil varnished shades of golden brown. He also made a quantity of good bows.

ERWIN E.J. *Bradford*
An amateur maker who made a quantity of instruments during the period about 1935-1955.

EVANS I.P. *Merthyr Tydfil*
He worked c. 1910 and made a number of quite good violins.

EVANS Thomas & Ralph *Shildon*
They worked together from about 1910 to 1930 and made some good violins based on the Guarnerius pattern covered with orange brown varnish.

EWAN David *Cowdenbeath*
Violin teacher, maker and repairer. His early instruments are highly arched but he soon corrected this failing and thereafter made his violins on a large Strad pattern. The backs etc. are generally of faintly figured wood and the fronts broad grained; the workmanship is excellent. He made about 100 violins and 20 'cellos. Label "Dd.Ewan/Cowdenbeath/1891". Sometimes he branded his name below the button.

EYLES Charles b.1850 *Harpenden & Wangford*
An artist who became interested in violin making and completed about 200 instruments of all types and of very reasonable workmanship and satisfactory tone. He worked from about 1890-1920.

EYLING Thomas *Gloucester*
He worked c. 1810 using the Amati model reasonably competently.

FALCONER W.H. *Perth*
An amateur maker who worked around the middle of the 19th century, his violins are on a large bodied model and not very distinguished.

FALKNER A. *London*
A professional flautist who worked as an amateur maker of no mean ability during the second quarter of the 20th century. He made both violins and violas the violins on the Strad model. His violas are of medium size - 415mm body length - and well made. Label "Arthur Falkner/Maker/London 1923".

FARRELL William James b.1870 *London*
He made his first instrument in 1916. He developed a system for making what he called the 'Truetone' violin and wrote a book about it. The main principle is strength, in fact the maker claimed that a man could stand on one of his violins made to the 'Truetone' principles without wrecking it, a most desirable characteristic as every musician will recognise. As regards to varnishing he advised makers to apply first three coats of coloured glue size to the bare wood followed by two coats of clear copal varnish!

FARRIMOND R. b.1870 *London*
A professional double bass player who had a violin shop and made a few very satisfactory violins.

FEAR Harry b.1878 *Handsworth*
An amateur maker who worked c. 1915, his work is quite good.

FELL Cyrus   *Leeds*

FELL William James b.1870   *London*
He worked in the Caledonian Road around the turn of the century and made
some attractive violins.

FENDT Bernhard b.Fussen 1769 d.London 1832   *London*
He came to London in 1798 having learned violin making from his uncle
Francois Fent in Paris. He worked for Thomas Dodd for eleven years and later
for John Betts. His work is seldom labelled with his name. He made some very
good double basses as well as all other instruments.

FENDT Bernhard Simon 1800-1852   *London*
Eldest son of Bernhard and his pupil He worked for Betts until 1832 and then in
partnership with Purdy later. He was a very fine imitator of old Italian masters
especially Guarnerius; even the labels are skillfully faked. His work is of a high order
and he was very prolific. In violins he favoured the Guarnerius model but many are
made on the Strad and other models. His best violas are on the Guarnerius model while
his 'cellos, which are very fine indeed, are on the Strad model with very few
exceptions. He also made double basses which are highly regarded. The varnish on his
instruments is sometimes applied to simulate age in a skillful manner. Some violins are
seen of Guarnerius model with a shiny red varnish attributed to B.S. Fendt, prospective
purchasers should exercise caution before buying.

FENDT Francis   *London & Liverpool*
Second son of Bernhard.

FENDT Jacob 1812-1849   *London*
Fourth son of Bernhard. He worked for Davis in Coventry St., and later for
Turner. He was a skillful copier and faker with labels to suit. Only a few
labelled "Jacob Fendt/London".

FENDT Martin 1812-1849   *London*
Third son of Bernhard. Worked with his father at Bett's establishment continuing
there after his father's death. His instruments are seldom labelled with his name.

FENDT William 1833-1852   *London*
Son of B.S. Fendt. He made some very fine instruments but there are few of
them. Label "William Fendt Jun/London 1851".

FERGUSON J.   *Edinburgh*
An amateur maker first quarter 20th century.

FERGUSON William   *Edinburgh*
He worked from about 1790-1820 and made some quite good instruments
including 'cellos.

FERRIER William b.1849   *Dundee*
An amateur maker who made a large number of instruments of good
workmanship but the models which he chose are often unsuitable and in
others the plate thicknesses are incorrect. It is a pity that such good work did
not achieve a better result.

FIDLER J. died c.1958 *Reading*
He was an amateur maker who was taught by C.S. Willis. He made a few violins of average merit.

FIELDING –. *Canley, Coventry*
He worked about 1960 and in addition to making violins made several violas on the Tertis pattern then in vogue.

FINDLAY James 1815-1896 *Pandanaram*
He was an amateur maker from about 1929. His work is variable in quality but only from of average merit downwards. The wood of his violins is plain, the purfling (when present) is wide but cleanly put in, the varnish thin and rather a nondescript yellow brown in colour. He is reputed to have made over 500 instruments following the Guarnerius or Stradivarius pattern principally. The tone is generally good.

FINDLAY William c.1860 *Leicester*

FINGLAND Samuel *Glasgow*
He was an amateur maker during the last quarter 19th century.

FIRTH George I *Leeds*
He was a pupil of William Booth Senior and worked at 110 Briggate Leeds but not very successfully.

FIRTH George II *Bradford*
He worked from about 1870-1880 and his work is very similar to that of his father, that is not very good.

FIRTH Thomas George b.1869 *Plumstead*
He took up violin making late in life as an amateur maker but had a good instructor in William Robinson. His instruments are larger in body that those of his teacher but they are well made and have an excellent tone. They are well varnished with a deep golden brown oil varnish and the handsome woods give them an attractive appearance.

FISHER George c.1815 *Cheltenham*

FISHER Leslie H. b.1904 *Wallasey*
He was apprenticed to Rushworth & Dreaper from 1921/1922 and worked for them until 1933 during which time he made some of the 'Ardeton' instruments. He also made some personally labelled violins which are on the Strad pattern some of which were left unvarnished. Label "Leslie H.Fisher/Maker/Wallasey Ches.1930/Muriel".

FIVAZ Charles F. *London*
He worked in the Essex Road, Islington from about 1870 to 1900, it is not known who might have been his teacher but his work is first class and closely resembles the best French makers: it is well set off by an excellent oil varnish which has an orange red/brown shade. Label "Charles Fivaz.Teluti/Fecit A.D. 1892. London".

FLECK William 1852-1914   *High Wycombe*
A Doctor of medicine who made some good instruments, violins, violas and 'cellos. The violins are mostly on the Strad model, they are made from choice woods and nicely varnished. He was assisted by his wife who also made some good instruments and completed and varnished those left by her husband on his death.

FLEMING John   *Saltcoats*
He worked from about 1870 to 1900 on the Strad model. His violins are unlabelled but his name FLEMING is branded under the button.

FLECHER Joseph c.1810   *Hitchin*

FORD Jacob   *London*
He worked in London from about 1770-1795. His instruments have a moderately high arching which is a sort of cross between Stainer and Amati. The work is very good the edges being particularly well worked and without too pronounced a grooving between the edge and the rise of the modelling. The purfling is well inserted, the centre strip (in common with many English makers of the period) being pronouncedly white between two thin black strips. The backs etc. are mostly well figured and this is small and frequently horizontal, the varnish rather hard but good and in golden brown or brown shades. In addition to a label he often signed his name inside the table. Label "J. Ford Maker/South Street, Grosvenor Square/London 1780". "J.Ford Maker/The corner of Davis Street and Berkeley Square/London".

FORD William b.1904   *Sunderland*
He was a joiner who taught himself to make violins and made some good instruments on classical lines, the workmanship is satisfactory and they are nicely varnished.

FORREST A.   *Edinburgh*
He worked c. 1830. He made very satisfactory violins, the workmanship careful, scroll rather large and wide yet neatly carved, purfling carefully inlaid, the modelling rather full, table thickness too great at the centre, tone sweet but not powerful, golden varnish. Not labelled but written inside "A. Forrest/Edinburgh/1830".

FORREST W.   *Whitburn*
An amateur maker who worked c. 1920.

FORRESTER Alexander   *Fauldhouse*
He worked as an amateur c. 1950 and made some quite good violins. He used to sell his "semi-flexible purfling cut and dressed ready for bedding" to other makers.

FORSTER Edward   *Blyth & Bournemouth*
He was a self taught amateur maker who claimed to be a descendant of the famous family but this does not show up in his work which at best is tolerable but includes some wildly eccentric instruments made from unconventional woods and patterns. He worked from about 1935-1960.

FORSTER Joseph   *Carlisle*
Son of William I. A professional 'cellist who made a few instruments.

FORSTER John   *Brampton*
He made a few rough violins Stainer style, unpurfled and with dark brown varnish.

FORSTER Simon Andrew 1810-1870   *London*
Son of William III and his pupil. The quality of his violins varies considerably but there is no doubt that he was capable of turning out good clean work when he chose to do so but some of his violins are poor by any standards. The violas are small but generally made quite well with, often, long hooky corners. 'Cellos are his best instruments and these are just under 735mm body length and made from good spruce and prettily figured maple, the workmanship is good, they are neatly purfled and well varnished either red/brown or orange/brown - sometimes the varnish has developed a slight crackle. The tone is not all that might be expected probably due to the excessive thickness of the table at the centre; quite commonly this is 5.5mm centrally tapering to 2.5mm at the edges. Label "S.A. Forster/Violin, tenor and Violoncello Maker/No.17 London" also signed inside the table S.A. Forster/No. 17/London and further signed above the tailpin.

FORSTER William I 1714-1801   *Brampton*
Son of John. He made a few violins a little better than his father's on much the same pattern and unpurfled. Label "William Forster/Violin Maker/in Brampton".

FORSTER William II 1739-1808   *London*
Known as 'Old Forster' or 'Royal Forster'. He was taught by his father William I and came to London in 1759 and gained employment in a music shop: there he did well and soon set up his own establishment in 1762, subsequently he worked from St. Martin's Lane and later 348 The Strand. Assisted by workmen he produced three classes of violins; the cheapest not purfled, plain woods and cheap quality varnish, the second class purfled, better materials and varnish and the third the best of everything. In the best instruments the style is a sort of Amati with the body length rarely exceeding 352mm, the backs nicely flamed, tables narrow grained, the corners often long and hooky, and the varnish red/brown or orange/brown. Violas are similar but the body length - 382mm - too small for true viola tone. 'Cellos are his best works and some are excellent. the proportions are full although the body length rarely exceeds 735mm or just under (very occasionally 750mm), the pegbox tapers quickly and has a big heel to match the button, the soundholes are rather open and often set sloping slightly inwards giving a 'knock-kneed' effect to them, the varnish, dark red or golden brown, sometimes has crackled. 'Cellos have the number and the date written under the tailgut. Various labels were used sometimes with plenty of wording and others simply "William Forster".

FORSTER William III 1764-1824   *London*
Known as 'Young Forster'. His best work is very like that of his father's. Assisted by workmen he produced four classes of violins and it is said that the cheapest sold for nine shillings (45p). His best instruments are his 'cellos which are more on Stradivarius lines than his fathers, these too are often signed above the tailpin.

FORSTER William IV 1788-1824   *London*
Pupil of William II and William III and also worked with Thomas Kennedy. He made only about 12 or 15 violins, this small number being accounted for by the fact that he was a professional violinist and died so young. His few instruments show that he was capable of good work.

FOSTER Richard P. c.1924   *Maldon*

FOSTER Robert C. c.1925   *Lancaster*

FOWERS Herbert b.1868   *Draycott*
He was a pupil of Frank Howard and made violins, violas and 'cellos. The violins
are on the Strad model, the workmanship is good and they are nicely varnished a
deep red/brown. Label "Made by/Herbert Fowers/Draycott, near Derby.1925".

FOX Joseph   *Leeds*
He worked circa 1860 as an amateur but his work is very good and covered
with an excellent varnish.

FOX Richard   *Enfield*
A piano technician who worked as an amateur violin maker c. 1920. He made some
excellent violins on the Strad model. There was some collaboration with Percy Lee of
Cricklewood since I have seen a 'cello with their printed joint label dated 1924.

FRANCIS Thomas R.   *Mendelsham, Suffolk*
It is presumed that he was an amateur maker but his work is good. The model
he used is that of Stradivarius, the materials well chosen and the varnish a deep
red just slightly crazing. His No. 30 dated 1884.

FRANKLAND -   *London*
He was a pupil of William Forster III c. 1785. He worked at Robin Hood Court,
Shoe Lane and was employed by Forster II and Forster III as an outworker.

FRANKS Raymond   *London*
He made several violins of good workmanship c. 1950 as an amateur and also
taught violin making at the Northern Polytechnic from about 1951-1954 when
he left the country for America.

FREEMAN G. c.1940   *Harpenden*

FRYER John Charles   *York*
Known only by a 'cello dated 1821 of 750mm body length, one piece slab back
handsomely figured, well made, upright soundholes, very broad purfling,
golden brown varnish and signed on the inner back.

FROST Joseph   *Spittlehouse*
He worked c. 1830, amateur work of average merit, yellow varnish.

FULTON Henry   *Liverpool*
He worked c. 1900 and made violins and 'cellos which are quite good.

FURBER David   *London*
The first of this well known family to have made violins. He worked c. 1760-
1780 having been taught by John Johnson. His violins are on the Stainer style
and not very great. He worked a good deal for the trade and his name is
sometimes found inside the tables written in pencil.

FURBER Henry John   *London*
He worked c. 1880 and his work is excellent. The violins are on the Strad
model and well made but frequently from plainish wood. The violas are fine - of
420mm body length and with a good outline, the pegbox finished with a 'cello
type heel. His instruments are seldom labelled but sometimes his name and a
date is written inside the table.

FURBER John   *London*
He worked from about 1810 to 1845 and is generally regarded as being the best
maker of the family. His violins mostly follow Amati but a few are on the Strad
model. The arching of the Amati violins is not accurately so since there is a
pronounced groove inside the purfling from which the arching rises. Thus the
arching under the bridge position is 'pinched' and this is detrimental to the
tone which is sweet but not powerful. Violas have similar characteristics and
are on the small side. The 'cellos are generally good, in these the arching is
better developed than in some of the violins. In addition to instruments bearing
his own name he worked for Betts as an outworker. His workshop moved
around and labels show him working from 13 St. John's Row (sometimes given
as John's Row), Turnmill Street and Cow Cross, Smithfield.

FURBER James   *London*
According to a label he worked with his brother Matthew - "James & Matthew
Furber/Clerkenwell Green 1796".

FURBER Matthew I d. circa 1790   *London*
He was the son of David Furber and was taught violin making by his father.

FURBER Matthew II d.1831   *London*
The second son of Matthew I and his pupil. He worked from about 1780-1831 at
various addresses - No. 1 Pool Terrace City Road; Cowcross Street, near opposite
Booth's the Distillery; Clerkenwell Green and 77 Turnmill Street, Brick Lane. He
was a prolific maker and his instruments are often very good; the violins are on
differing models and the arching is better than that of his more famous brother.
The workmanship not first rate but quite acceptable and the varnish, a darkish
yellow or reddish/brown is of good quality. He made violins, violas and 'cellos.

FURBER William   *London*
He worked about 1820-1840 but not very well.

FURLOUGH Henry   *Bath*
He worked about 1800-1830 on a sort of Amati style but the arching is flatter,
sometimes 'ink' purfling replaces the proper purfling, workmanship quite
good, rather nice golden varnish.

FURNOW Walter   *Cheltenham*
He worked c. 1800. His violins are highly arched and very ordinary.

FUSSEL Louis b.1925   *Bedford*
A violin/viola teacher who was taught violin making by George Webster. The
modelling of his violins is decidedly bulgy and the workmanship not good.
Reddish varnish thickly applied.

GABBITAS E.   *Sheffield*
Worked from about 1940-1970 and was well known as a careful repairer in the
Sheffield area. He also made a few violins and bows of good quality.

GADD Joseph J. b.1895   *Brough*
He took to violin making late in life as an amateur making his first violin in
1942. His instruments are quite well made.

GAFTETH Geoffrey
Late 17th century. His violins are highly built, ink lines instead of purfling, quite
well made, dark red varnish, sweet but weak tone.

GAIDA Giovanni b.1862   *London*
Although his tickets give Ivrea as his place of work to pander to the cult of
worshippers of Italian made violins most of his instruments were made just off the
Charing Cross Road. He came to this country in 1890 for five years then returned to
Italy and finally settled here in 1904 being employed by the Stainer Manufacturing Co.
and later by F.W. Chanot. He established his own workshop in 1925 in Castle Street,
Long Acre. His fine violins are modelled on the Strad pattern almost exclusively, the
materials and workmanship is always excellent, the varnish too looks nice but is
rather soft and wears away quickly, colours mostly deep orange brown or golden
brown. He made for London dealers such as Dykes and Withers and sometimes his
name, as maker, is mentioned on the respective firms labels. He made violas and
'cellos but few of them. Sometimes he branded G.GAIDA inside the back.

GAIDA Silvio Cyril 1889-1952   *London*
Son and pupil of the above. He was a professional musician with Troise and his
Mandoliers but helped his father with repairs at which he was adept and made
about a dozen violins of excellent workmanship. Label "Silvio Gaida figlio di
Giovanni 1930" (signed).

GARDEN James   *Edinburgh*
He worked during the last quarter of the 19th century as an amateur. He was a
professional violinist and made a few violins and violas in his spare time.

GARDINER Pierson   *London*
He worked from about 1760-1790. His violins are something like those of
Duke's Amati style but generally the backs and sides are more prettily marked.
They are seldom labelled but P. GARDINER is branded inside the back and/or
under the button.

GARDNER Charles   *London*
He worked circa 1780-1795 but his instruments are not very good.

GARDNER Hugo   *London*
He worked in Chelsea between about 1860-1880 making violins on both Strad
and Guarnerius models.

GARDNER Joseph   *Broxburn*
He worked c. 1820 as an amateur and the few violins which he made are
nothing much.

GARTH Reginald   *Kendal*
An amateur maker c.1870.

GASKIN George 1856-1913   *London*
A policeman who took up violin making as a hobby and succeeded at it. His violins are well made from good materials but they are a shade on the heavy side: they are varnished generally in various shades of yellow.

GAY Wilfred   *Bristol*
He worked c. 1910 and was taught by Henry Lye of Camerton. He did not make many instruments but those which he did were well made of good materials and sounded pleasant.

GEARY William   *London*
He was taught violin making by W.B Prince of Tooting and worked circa 1920. His violins are mainly on the Strad model although a few are in the style of Guarnerius. His materials are well chosen with finely flamed backs and ribs and this treated to meticulous workmanship, all this topped off by a good oil varnish nicely laid on and polished. He was taught bow making by L.T. Chappell of Forest Gate (who learned the craft from James Tubbs) and the bows he made were in the Tubbs style and, indeed, very close copies of them.

GIBBONS Arthur William b.1914   *Skeyton*
He was taught violin making by W.J. Piercy of Hanwell. He was mainly occupied by repairing for which he was much esteemed but also made a number of good violins which are usually varnished shades of golden brown.

GIBBS James   *London*
He worked at No. 2 New Street Lambeth from about 1800-1845 for better known makers and dealers mostly. No doubt he made some instruments under his own name but I have never seen any.

GIBSON Henry   *Liverpool*
He worked circa 1890 but his work is not at all good, it is however covered with a nice varnish.

GILBERT Jeffrey   *New Romney*
An amateur maker who made some good violins and 'cellos . He worked c. 1840-1870.

GILBERT Jeffrey James b.1850 *New Romney, Peterborough & Richmond*
Son of the above. He made about 40 instruments in New Romney. In some of these the edgework is very pronounced and the corners long, indeed overdone, with the purfling going to a long 'bee sting' but the overall workmanship is excellent and the woods well chosen. Violas from this period are too small for good viola tone (No. 18 dated 1884 very handsome but only 384mm body length and having poor tone on the bottom strings). He moved to Peterborough in 1886 and was still using up his New Romney labels in 1887 with the address altered to 32 Broad Bridge Street. His work now became very refined. The violins are on a personal model and 357mm or just under in body length, the violas 405mm (a few made measuring 432mm but they are too big for comfortable playing) and the 'cellos 755mm. The choice of woods is

excellent and his instruments are always made from handsomely figured hardwoods and perfectly straight grained spruce: the workmanship in every respect is first class. Only in varnishing has he had moments of failure for in some instruments, particularly deep red coatings, the varnish has crazed, sometimes very badly. The tonal quality of his work is very satisfactory.

GILCHRIST James 1832-1894   *Glasgow*
He made 90 instruments of mostly fine workmanship at 109 Hope Street, Glasgow but had taken up violin making late in life. His violins are on a model akin to Stradivarius but longer in the body, the backs and ribs are made from handsome wood and the workmanship is clean and sharp. The varnish he used is occasionally chippy and his best colours are a fine deep red, orange/brown and golden red. Label "James Gilchrist/Rothsay 1893". His instruments are not sufficiently appreciated.

GILKES Samuel 1787-1827   *London*
He was apprenticed to Charles Harris and later worked for a time with William Forster establishing his own workshop in 1810. His violins are of no particular model. Some are on Amati lines but flatter arched and some, the majority, on more Strad lines but not exactly so. He generally chose handsomely figured woods for the backs and ribs and the workmanship is excellent. The 'cellos are more on Strad lines but not so long in the body and the soundholes more open and set straight, scroll chamfers and edges blackened, handsomely figured maple and strongly grained fronts. His varnishes vary, some coatings are a fine deep red and very like Forsters but the majority are in shades of golden/brown. Sometimes his instruments are labelled and/or stamped GILKES inside (in the case of 'cellos often under the tailgut as well). He made a number of instruments for dealers into which various labels were placed (or none at all) but compared with his personally labelled work they are very second rate and only speculatively identifiable.

GILKES William 1811-1875   *London*
Son of Samuel and a prolific maker. He is especially renowned for his double basses but the remainder of his work, although at times very good, is not up to that of his father. His violins are often on the Maggini pattern and double purfled, but he made all models. The backs are generally of handsomely figured wood with the figure slanting upwards, the tables fine grained, the varnish, mostly shades of golden red, has sometimes crazed. he worked at various addresses. Label "W. Gilkes/Maker/14 Dartmouth Street/Westminster 1938". Sometimes branded "GILKS/Westminster/London".

GILL Lovett G.   *Walton on Thames & Odiham*
He was an architect who made about 40 instruments of good quality including several violas on the then popular 'Tertis' pattern for which he produced a set of plans which he sold to other makers. His instruments are dated from Walton on Thames in 1925 and later from Odiham, Hampshire (1940).

GIRVAN Thomas b.1847   *Edinburgh*
He was probably an amateur maker and the work is average. Label "Thomas Girvan/Edinburgh 1862".

GLENDAY James   *Pandanaram*
He was taught violin making by James Findlay but his work is not good.

GLENNIE William   *Aberdeen*
He worked for some time with John Marshall and also made some good
instruments bearing his own name.

GLENISTER William b.1850   *Watford & London*
He made about 200 instruments, violins, violas and 'cellos and the tone of these
is generally very good but the workmanship, while never lacking even to the
most critical, has, in certain aspects amateur touches about it. It is not known
from whom he received any instruction and therefore it is presumed that he
was a self taught amateur who had above average ability. Most of his violins are
on the Strad pattern but he made some following Guarnerius, the backs are
sometimes not highly figured but some are made with very handsome wood,
the arching frequently tends to be on the flat side, the edges thick and the oil
varnish - red brown and golden brown shades seem to have been preferred -
rather thickly applied and sometimes now tending to crackle. His 'cellos are
frequently quite large, 768mm, and often have long necks which makes the
playing of them difficult, they are rather heavy.

GLENISTER Edward J.   *Lincoln*
He worked from about 1930-1955 and was a professional violinist who made
some good violins and undertook repair work for the area in which he lived.

GLOAG John b.1852   *Galston*
His violins are modelled on the Strad pattern and quite well made. Label "John
Gloag/Galston/1898".

GOFTON Robert   *Whitby*
He worked from about 1860-1890 and made about 30 violins of quite reasonable
quality generally over long in the body. He was a cabinet maker by trade.

GOLDSMITH William   *Chelmsford*

GOODMAN James 19th century   *Brentford*

GORDON Hugh   *Belfast*
His work is variable in quality but the best of it is very neat. The model of his violins is
an original one, the woods used (in the best instruments) is of good figure generally
small, the edges nearly flat, the scroll well carved, the varnish thin and weak but the
tone good. Not always labelled but GORDON branded below the button.

GORDON Hugh   *Belfast*
Son of the above. Rather similar work to that of his father. Label "Made by
Hugh Gordon/(Son of the late Hugh Gordon, Stoneyford)/Violin Maker &
Repairer" also stamped GORDON on the button.

GORDON M.E.   *Plymouth*
A Doctor of medicine and amateur violin maker who made about 20
instruments of goodish workmanship circa 1940-1960.

GORRIE James   *Glasgow*
He worked circa 1895 as an amateur maker and built some good violins on the
Guarnerius pattern and these are varnished with a deep red varnish.

GORRIE Andrew   *Bonnybridge*
He worked circa 1900 as an amateur maker; his work is quite good.

GOSS Philip c.1860-1895   *Plymouth*

GOTHARD F. 19th century   *Huddersfield*

GOUGH John   *Thornbury*
He worked from about 1845 to 1870. His violins are nicely made on a pattern
near to Stradivarius using good materials. He also made violas and 'cellos the
latter being rather nice. Mostly the varnish is golden brown in colour. Some
instruments are stamped "J.GOUGH/THORNBURY".

GOUGH Walter   *Leeds*
His work is very ordinary, his working period being between about 1820-1840.
For a while he worked with Thomas Absam (q.v.).

GOULDING   *London*
A dealer who stamped his name on instruments made for him by others. Mostly
they are of Tyrolean origin but some are English. Some of the 'cellos stamped
with the name were made by Thomas Kennedy. Sometimes his instruments are
labelled "Goulding & Co./20 Soho Square,London" but more frequently just
stamped with the name under the button.

GOWERTH John Mid 18th century   *Oxford*

GRAHAM William   *Wicklow - Eire*
An amateur maker who worked from about 1925-1940 but had limited ability.

GRAHAM R.   *Cadoxton*
He was taught violin making by James Meek, his few violins are said to be good.

GRATER Thomas   *Birmingham*
He worked in Ryland Street from about 1874 to 1925 and was a prolific maker
of violins, violas and 'cellos as well as carrying out repairs. He made some
excellent instruments covered with a fine oil varnish which he made himself.
His violins are frequently on the Guarnerius pattern but he made others as
"copies" of classical masters; some of the violins have the sides and back of the
pegbox carved in floral relief and very well done too - if you like that sort of
decoration. Towards the end of his working period he ceased to make his own
varnish and used that made by Millington.

GRAY J. c.1820   *London*

GRAY John   *Fochabers*
He worked from about 1860-1875 and made a few violins of average merit as an
amateur maker.

GRAY John d.1950   *Sunderland*
He was a maker and repairer. He made about 30 instruments - violins violas and
'cellos - using good materials and with careful workmanship and good results. In
some instruments the varnish has not worn well and is badly crackled.

GREENWOOD G.W. b. 1885 *Manchester & Rochdale*
He was apprenticed to and later worked for Thomas Hesketh, then in 1912 set up his own establishment in Rochdale. His violins are on Guarnerius and Strad patterns, he used handsome wood for the backs and sides and good pine for the tables and the workmanship is always excellent. The varnish generally red/brown or golden/brown well laid on and nicely polished. His instruments certainly bear favourable comparison with his master's.

GREGSON Robert b.1871 *Blackburn*
He was a professional maker who made about 100 violins and violas on Stradivarian lines with good workmanship. His label is printed within a lined border "Arte et Labore/Robert Gregson/Blackburn. Anno 1908".

GREY George & Andrew *Dundee*
Father and son who worked circa 1915.

GRIBBEN P.J. *Dalmuir*
An amateur maker who worked c. 1930, his work is of average merit.

GRIFFIN William *Blackheath*
An amateur maker who made some violins on the Guarnerius pattern reasonably well and varnished them orange/red.

GRIFFITHS A.V. c.1920 *London*

GRICE John *Edinburgh*
According to his label he came to work in Edinburgh from London, during the early part of the 18th century. His violins are well made on the Strad model from handsome wood and nicely varnished golden brown.

GRIERSON Samuel *Wishaw*
Probably an amateur maker who worked during the first quarter 20th century. His work is of average merit.

GRIME Harold c.1910 *Accrington*

GRIMES R. 19th century *Sherborne*

GUITON R. *Cork*
An amateur maker who worked from about 1890-1910. His violins are modelled after Strad and Guarnerius and they are nicely made.

GUNTER Henry *Scarborough*
He worked c. 1850 but not very well.

GURNSEY C.J. b. 1875 *London*
His output was small, he being occupied with repairing, but what there is of it is quite good.

GWYTHER Henry *Gloucester*
He worked c. 1840, his work is rough.

GUY Henry *London*
He worked c. 1925 and his work is very reasonable.

HAINSWORTH Charles c.1920 *Norwich*

HALES Herbert b.1883 *Coventry*
He was mainly a repairer but also made a few violins of fair quality.

HALL William *Oldham*
He worked at 78 Morris Street, Glodwick, Oldham between about 1880 and 1914. His violins are made on Stradivarius, Guarnerius and Amati models but principally the first. They are made from good materials treated to good workmanship and very nicely varnished. His output was small.

HAMBLETON Joseph c.1850 *Salford*

HAMILTON William *Uddingstone*
He was an engineer by profession. In the last quarter of the 19th century he made a number of violins and violas of good workmanship. The violins are in the style of Stradivarius and attractively oil varnished.

HAMILTON W.T.R. c.1910 *Edinburgh*

HAMMETT Thomas b.1872 *Plumstead*
From the style of his work he may well have been instructed by William Robinson; his work is excellent, the violins are on the Strad pattern using handsome woods and made with careful workmanship, the edges and corners attractively worked, soundholes well cut, in fact everything is done with precision: his instruments have a good sound. He used a written label in old English lettering.

HAMMOND John b. 1870 *West Burton Wensleydale*
He was a self taught amateur who made about 25 instruments which are of above average workmanship. Label "John Hammond/West Burton, Wensleydale/Fecit 1949".

HANCOCK Arthur James b.1851 *Stoke on Trent*
An amateur maker who made about 20 finely finished instruments.

HANCOCK George b. 1851 *Stoke on Trent*
He was a professional maker and repairer from 1886. His violins are made on both Stradivarius and Guarnerius patterns skillfully handled. His output was small.

HANDLEY Henry b.1839 *Worcester*
As a professional maker and repairer he made 106 violins, 6 violas and 2 'cellos up to his retirement in 1927. He used both classical patterns and an original model for his violins, some of the latter are over long in the body. His work is on the whole satisfactory but inclined to be on the heavy side. The varnish is generally in shades of brown and some coatings have developed crazing. Printed label "Henry Handley/Fiddle Restorer and Maker/ Worcester/1918 No. 98".

HANSON Albert *Huddersfield*
He was the proprietor of a large music shop in Huddersfield. Instruments c. 1930 are seen labelled with his name as are bows stamped ALBERT HANSON. The instruments appear to be individual work and are of good quality, the bows are excellent. The puzzle is did he make them, have them made to order for his establishment or buy them 'in the white' and varnish them? The appearance makes me think that these are English instruments and bows and the probability is that they were made to order – in any event, they are good.

HANCOX Arthur J. *Deddington*
He was a pupil of A.J. Roberts and worked at Deddington c.1920. His violins are nicely made on the Strad model and generally varnished in shades of red/brown.

HARBOUR Jacob *London*
He worked from about 1760-1790. His violins are highly arched and none too well made with straight set ugly soundholes, a poorly carved scroll, ink lines (or nothing at all) replace the purfling and all this covered by a dark 'floorboard' type varnish. He made some 'cellos which are better built but still not very good.

HARBOUR William *London*
He was the brother of Jacob and, working at about the same period, made a similar style of instrument.

HARDAY Henry c.1780 *London*

HARDIE Alexander 1777-1852 *Maxweltown*
He was an amateur maker of violins but one who was used to making things from wood. His output was not large, the violins are rather big in the body and the workmanship not very good, neither are they very well varnished. Branded HARDIE below the button.

HARDIE Alexander 1811-1890 *Galashields*
Son of the above and his work is very similar to that of his father.

HARDIE James *Edinburgh*
He worked at Edinburgh from about 1830-1855. His violins are very similar in model and style to those of Matthew Hardie to whom he was not related. He was by training a patternmaker. The workmanship is excellent, edges well raised but a trifle thick, purfling carefully laid in, well carved scroll and soundholes; he was rewarded by getting a good sound from his instruments.

HARDIE James 1836-1916 *Edinburgh*
Not related to the previous entry he was a grandson of Peter Hardie of Dunkeld. He is credited with making over 2,000 instruments, many of them being violins on the Maggini pattern, having made his first one in 1846 thus working for nearly 70 years. His early work is variable but the best can be very good indeed; it is a pity that so many of the violins are on a model which has fallen out of favour. He also made violas, 'cellos and double basses but these are not often seen. The varnish on early instruments is not too good but later ones are varnished with an oil varnish of good texture but a little chippy, red/brown and golden/brown shades being favoured.

HARDIE John   *Edinburgh*
He worked c. 1870 at 29A Broughton Street.

HARDIE Matthew 1775-1826   *Edinburgh*
His violins are something along the lines of the Strad model but not copies in
the strict sense of the word. Even in his early work his ability is apparent and
even though some may have been made quickly of not very impressive
materials, ink lines instead of purfling etc. the style is still good. His best violins
are good although the varnish is not up to the standard of the woodwork. The
tone is not always so satisfactory since it is often loud with little sweetness in it.
He made violas, some of these are so small, scarcely 380mm, as to be tonally
unsatisfactory but the larger ones are excellent. His 'cellos are scarce they are a
good size - 752mm - on the lines of a Stradivarius and sound well.

HARDIE Peter 1775-1863   *Dunkeld*
His violins are rather highly modelled on the Amati outline and are fairly well
made, mostly the backs are of small figure, and the fronts of medium width
pine both competently purfled. The scrolls are well cut but the channels either
side of the centre line are deeply cut and this, coupled with a greater width
than usual, spoils to some extent their appearance. He also made violas and
'cellos and the latter are particularly liked. His instruments are not labelled but
P. HARDIE is stamped on the back under the button.

HARDIE Thomas 1802-1856   *Edinburgh*
The son of Matthew and his pupil. His violins are on the same model as his
father's, the workmanship and general appearance is better but they have been
criticised by many for not sounding well. The wood of the backs and ribs is
more highly figured than those which Matthew made and in varnishing his
varnish is superior. These remarks apply to his best violins but he made others,
no doubt for a cheap sale, which are not in the same class. He made violas and
'cellos and the latter are well spoken of.

HARDING R.   *London*
A Hill's bowmaker who left them in 1956.

HARDWICK John Edward 1886-1966   *Ashstead*
By trade a wood carver and, being taught by G. Wulme-Hudson, the
constructional aspects of violin making were never a problem. His 'straight'
instruments are quite good but these seem to be few and he wasted his time on
making ornamented violins not at all artistically designed and in some instances
quite tasteless, often these instruments have variations in the colour of the
varnish from back to front.

HARDY D.   *Pocklington*
He made and repaired instruments about 1820.

HARE, John   *London*
He worked between about 1680 and 1710 first in Freeman's Yard and later at the
'Viol and Flute' near the Royal Exchange. Most of his violins are on a highly built
model following, but not attaining, the Stainer pattern; they are in fact not very
good. Some that he made are different in style, flat in model and long in the body;
some critics have conjectured that he might have worked with Daniel Parker.

HARE Joseph *London*
He worked between about 1700 and 1730. The son and pupil of John he was a better maker than his father. He worked at several addresses in or about Cornhill. His violins are large with flattish arching and the workmanship is good. The varnish is of good quality and generally a golden brown colour.

HARFORD Patrick *Dublin*
His rather good looking instruments were made around 1740.

HARFIELD Albourne E. *Southampton*
He worked as an amateur maker (he was a well known professional violinist and teacher) around the years 1910-1935. He made a quantity of satisfactory violins (other instruments not known) having a Stradivarius pattern and good quality red/brown varnish. His printed label shows his portrait with rows of violins in the background. His son, Bernard, continued as an amateur repairer and dealer.

HARRIS Charles I *London*
He worked from about 1780-1815. It is not known who taught him violin making and although employed as a Customs House official he produced a large number of instruments and the quality and productivity puts him in the professional class. His violins are principally on the Strad model but he also copied Amati, the materials are of good quality, the workmanship fine and the varnish either a rich ruddy brown or shades of golden brown. His 'cellos are particularly liked and are probably his best work. His name is often signed inside the table.

HARRIS Charles II *London, Steeple Aston, Adderbury, Woodstock*
Son and pupil of the above he worked with his father, then for John Hart and in 1824 moved to Oxfordshire where his instruments are labelled from various addresses. His work is not so good as that of his father nevertheless it is quite satisfactory. Both the violins and 'cellos are often long in the body and the model a hybrid one combining features from other patterns. The varnish is generally in shades of yellow brown and not particularly attractive

HARRIS John Edward b.1860 *Shildon & Gateshead*
He was a pupil of George Chanot in London. He made about 200 instruments of excellent workmanship using best quality woods and varnished with his own oil varnish. This varnish "Real Amber Oil Varnish-Eureka" he sold to other makers, it was very good but exhibited very variable drying qualities, it did not disappear from the market until about 1968 since his son Ernest continued to make and sell it. Printed label "Made by/J.E. Harris/Violin Maker/Nile Street, Gateshead. No. 39 Model 1913".

HARRIS Gordon 1925-1991 *London*
He was a pupil of P. Naysmyth at the London College of Furniture Trades. He made 31 violins, 31 violas (mostly 405mm body length), 4 'cellos and some replica old instruments. His work is generally good but not of professional quality. He undertook a good deal of repair work and dealt in old instruments and bows. He was a good water colour painter and poet.

HARGRaVE William *Manchester*
He worked about 1890 probably as an amateur; his small output is quite well made.

HARROD Jack d.1890 *Burton-on-Trent*
He was an amateur maker who completed several violins of average merit.

HART George b.1860 *London*
The son of John Thomas Hart. He made only a few violins and is better remembered as a collector and connoisseur of old instruments. Label "Made by George Hart/Crawford Street, 18**".

HART George b.1860 *London*
The son of the preceding. He was trained in Paris but made few instruments himself. His firm employed a number of able workmen who made replicas of famous instruments, these are made from the choicest woods with impeccable workmanship, finely full edges yet not overdone, beautifully inlaid purfling, finely cut soundholes and scroll and all covered by a capital oil varnish of rich texture in shades of orange brown and golden brown. Each instrument numbered and dated (No. 36 dated 1894 and No. 257 dated 1926 gives some idea of the productivity of the firm). The firm also made bows although not all of those stamped HART or HART & SON were made in their workshops.

HART Harold J. c.1945 *Exeter*

HART John Thomas 1805-1874 *London*
He was a pupil of Gilkes and made a few instruments of reasonable merit on the Amati pattern but achieved success as a restorer and expert dealer. Label "John Hart/Maker/14 Princes Street, Leicester Square/London, anno 18**".

HARVEY Ernest *Penarth & Cardiff*
He was an amateur maker who worked from about 1880 to 1905.

HARVEY Eugene *Dinas Powys*
Son of the above and also an amateur maker.

HARVEY Robert *Berwick on Tweed*
An amateur maker who worked from about 1830 to 1856.

HARWOOD J.A. *Newcastle on Tyne*
Little is known of this maker who from his label worked at 59 Oban Road, Newcastle circa 1920.

HASLAM W.D. *Croydon*
He was a Doctor of medicine who, as a violin maker, was self taught. He made a good number of violins, most of these being on the Strad model using good materials and this treated to the neatest work. He also made a few violins more highly arched, double purfled and not up to the quality of the Strad copies. The varnish is an oil varnish in shades of golden brown, sometimes crackled.

HAWES William   *Northampton*
I have seen no instruments made by him but have seen several bearing the
inscription "Attuned by William Hawes, Northampton and guaranteed to retain
the true Italian tone if the instrument is unaltered". These appeared during the
period 1920-1930.

HAXTON George b.1878   *Glasgow*
He was a self taught maker who established himself at 15 Roy Street, Glasgow
in 1910. His violins are modelled after Guarnerius mostly but a few follow
Stradivarius. The materials and workmanship are good and he covered his
instruments with a satisfactory oil varnish in red/brown or golden/brown
shades. Label "George Haxton/ 15 Roy Street/Glasgow/A.D. 1923 No. 56".

HAY James b.1869   *Guildford*
An amateur maker who worked from about 1915-1935, his work is fairly good.

HAYNES H. b.1867   *Great Malvern & Southsea*
He made a large number of violins on the Guarnerius pattern. These are good
both in workmanship and tone.

HAYNES Jacob   *London*
Fairly good work on the Stainer pattern circa 1750.

HAYNES & Co.   *London*
This firm operated from about 1880-1900. They employed workmen and put
the firm's label in their productions, some are good. Label "Haynes fecit 1897
No. 37/at 14 Grays Inn Road, London". The violins labelled the "Carrodus"
were made for them in Mirecourt and are of good quality.

HAYNES Jacob   *London*
He worked about 1750 making violins on a bulgy approximation to the Stainer
pattern.

HEAPS John K.   *Leeds*
He worked circa 1850 and, while possessing a good deal of ability, wasted
much of this talent by adopting theories in the constructional methods which
failed to produce what he desired. Thus while his violins look good they do not
come up to expectations as regards to their sound. His 'cellos are better.

HEARNSHAW Francis   *Nottingham*
He was a self taught amateur maker who worked from about 1880 to 1910. His
violins are on the pattern of a large Strad body length 362mm, the workmanship is
quite good and the orange brown varnish carefully laid on. Manuscript label.

HEATON William   *Gomersal, Leeds*
He worked during the last quarter of the 19th century and some years into the
20th. His violins are principally made on the Strad pattern but he also tried
both Guarnerius and Amati; in all of these the patterns are not faithfully copied.
The materials are always of good quality although the backs not always highly
figured, the arching tends to be flattish, edges strong and well rounded,
purfling excellent, scroll carving good but often the width from eye to eye is
excessive, the varnish an oil preparation in shades of golden brown and

occasionally red. He made about 200 violins (No. 157 dated 1900) and also made some good 'cellos. Label "William Heaton/Maker/Hill Top,Gomersal/Nr. Leeds" - the number and date added.

HEBDEN Herbert *West Green, London*
A little known maker who produced some excellent violins first quarter 20th century.

HEESOM Edward *London*
He worked around 1750. He copied Stainer in the English fashion, that is the violins are much more bulgy. The backs are generally well figured, frequently there is no purfling (but some have been purfled later), the edges are sharply raised, soundholes upright and rather open and the nicks are large. He made both violins and violas. Many are not labelled but stamped HEESOM below the button.

HEINRICH Otto *Bath*
He was a professional violinist who had a large teaching practice in Bath. He made some very nice violins on the Strad model between the years 1900 and 1920.

HENDERSON D.G. *Edinburgh*
He worked during the last quarter 19th century and was an amateur maker. His violins are made on the Strad model of good materials and excellent workmanship, generally varnished shades of red. Manuscript label.

HENDERSON John b1842 *Broxburn*
He worked during the last quarter 19th century and made some good violins. He exhibited some at Edinburgh and Glasgow and won medals for them.

HENDERSON David *Aberdeen*
19th century. His work is not very good.

HENLEY William b1870 *Lee*
An amateur maker who received some help from J.Holder and made a few rather nice violins as an amateur.

HENSTRIDGE William H. b1882 *Highams Park & Tiverton*
He was a pupil of Werro in Berne, and a professional violinist. He made a number of good violins as an amateur on the Strad and Guarnerius models using excellent materials and with good workmanship. They were rather well 'wooded' and the tone is consequently subdued. M/S label "Wm. H. Henstridge/London, Fecit 1921".

HERRING H. *Gloucester*
He worked circa 1865.

HESKETH Thomas Earle 1866 - 1952 *Manchester*
He was a pupil of G.A. Chanot and continued to work for him until 1891 when he set up on his own at 23 Lower Mosley Street. His violins are principally modelled on Guarnerius but he made on an original model as well as copying Stradivarius and Ruggeri: he is however best known for his "Facsimile copies" of Joseph Guarnerius del Gesu. Some of these instruments were made in whole or part by Paul Arne Voigt. His violas are 400mm, 410mm and many after a fine Amati viola 422mm. He made very few 'cellos. All his work is of the highest order material of the best quality and the varnish fine.

HEWITT A.W. *Shanklin*
He worked c. 1900 as an amateur maker.

HEWITT John 1733 - 1798 *Feltham*
He was a minister of the Church and made a few violins on the Stainer pattern of nice apperarance.

HEWITT Richard 18th century *Manchester*

HEYES Thomas *Charnock Richards*
He was an amateur maker who worked c. 1930; average ability.

HICKMAN F. *Leytonstone*
He worked c. 1920 as an amateur maker. His work is very clean and precise and gives the impression that he was a trained cabinet maker. He used various patterns for his violins and some are on a Maggini pattern of normal body length, double purfled and varnished golden brown.

HICKS George Herbert b1886 *Oxford*
He first worked for G.A. Chanot in Manchester and later opened his own shop in Market Street, Oxford in 1910. He made Strad modelled violins of good quality but generally over the normal body length. He was esteemed for good repair work.

HIGSON Daniel 1849 - 1906 *Ashton on Ribble*
An amateur maker who made about 30 violins on the Strad model with fair workmanship and tonal success. M/S label.

HILL Alfred Ebsworth 1862 - 1940 *London*
He was the third son of William Ebsworth and was taught violin making first by his father then in Mirecourt. He made few instruments himself since his entire working life was taken up by running the famous firm of W.E. Hill & Sons and in establishing their workshops. He devoted much time to experiments with varnish and some of these were used on instruments made in the Hill workshops: unfortunately some of his recipes were not successful and the coatings have worn badly.

HILL Henry Lockey 1774 - 1835 *London*
He was the son and pupil of Lockey Hill. He worked for John Betts for some years then on his own account from several addresses around the Borough area - Market Street, 7 Brandon Row, and Kent Street. His violins are mostly on the Strad model and generally the work is of fine quality although they are not always made from handsome woods. He also made some good violas 405mm body length and a good number of 'cellos which are on the small side (736mm body length) following the general ideas of the time. His varnish is often pale in colour, golden yellow might best describe it but occasionally we see a deeper coloured instrument in an orange/red shade.

HILL Hugh *Belfast*
He was an amateur maker who worked c. 1910 and made about thirty instruments which are good.

HILL Joseph   *Penn, Wolverhampton & Paignton*
He was a skilful amateur maker. He worked in the motor car industry on
wooden bodies and made violins and violas as a hobby during the period 1925 -
1960: one dated 1933 being a splendid copy of the Alard Strad. Later he retired
to Paignton and was employed by Harris, Osborne & Co. on piano casework as
well as undertaking violin repairs.

HILL Joseph I. 1715 - 1784   *London*
He was apprenticed to Peter Wamsley. His violins are on the Amati pattern and
have a fairly full arching with the soundholes set straight, a little on the long
side and not particularly elegant. His violas are often too small (378mm) for
serious use but he also made some of 400mm body length which are good, in
pattern they are much like the violins. 'Cellos are his best instruments and
some are really good, they vary in size from 735mm to 750mm and it is among
the larger ones that his best 'cellos are found. His varnish is good generally in
shades of golden yellow or golden brown.

HILL Joseph II 1747 - 1793   *London*
Second son of Joseph I. He assisted his father until the latter's death in1784; a
few instruments are known personally signed after that date.

HILL Joseph III 1815 - 1837   *London*
A son of Henry Lockey Hill. He is not mentioned in any previous records as a
maker yet a violin has been seen labelled "J. Hill Maker/Son of the late L.
Hill/London 1837".

HILL Lockey 1756 - 1810   *London*
Fourth son of Joseph I and his pupil. His work is good but not outstanding and
generally covered with a nondescript brownish shade of varnish. His 'cellos are
around 735mm body length mostly of nicely figured wood but occasionally with
plain backs and open grained fronts; he made some 'cellos for Norris & Barnes.
A characteristic of his instruments is that the purfling is wider than usual with a
very white strip between; two narrow black strips. He used various labels e.g.
"Hill/Violin and Violoncello Maker/No. 70 Kent St., Boro'/London".

HILL John   *London*
A little known maker who worked around 1700.

HILL William 1745 - 1790   *London*
He was the eldest son of Joseph I. His violins are in the Amati style with rather
prominent corners, violas, of 400mm body length, are very similar. His varnish
is of excellent quality and golden yellow in colour. The tone is of good quality
and little power. He used various labels e.g. "Willm Hill/maker in Poland
Street/near Broad Street Carnaby Market/1772".

HILL William Ebsworth 1817 - 1895   *London*
He was the son of Henry Lockey and his pupil afterwards working with both
his father and brother Joseph II. Later he worked for Charles Harris II in Oxford
returning to London in 1838 and establishing himself at 29 St. George's Road,
West Square, Southwark. He made relatively few instruments and many of
these not so good as one might expect. Most of these were made at Southwark
and, from a label, it appears that he was working there in 1853. Probably his

violas are his best works, these are of large pattern, 416mm body length at a time when most English violas were too small, and made from handsome materials, the soundholes are not too good however, set very straight, far too open and with a wide gap between the lower wing and the continuation of the table. 'Cellos are 745mm body length with the outline either side of the button and at the bottom rather straight and the inner bouts too short. His fame really rests in the founding and consolidation of the firm of W.E. Hill & Sons into what few would doubt was the greatest ever firm in the violin trade.

HILL Paul Ebsworth 1896 - 1968   *London*
He was the son of William Henry Hill and apprenticed to A. Delanoy in Bordeaux. He remained with the firm of W.E. Hill & Sons until his retirement in 1960 actually participating in both making and restoring instruments.

W.E. HILL & Sons   *London*
Established in 1887 this firm became the World's leading firm of violin specialists and acknowledged experts on old instruments. They built workshops at Hanwell where new instruments and bows were made and old instruments restored and repairs carried out by a staff of trained workmen. Violins bearing their name are made from the choicest materials with impeccable workmanship and these are all numbered and dated e.g. No. 24 dated 1890 and No. 523 dated 1973. Violins, violas and 'cellos were made. Sometimes the varnish, particularly of those made just before the first World War has crazed badly. As bow makers too they were famous. The best seasoned pernambuco wood only was used and this fashioned into bows by a staff of workmen trained in their own workshops and with careful selection a very even standard of quality was preserved: only one criticism can be made namely that some bows - particularly for the 'cello - are really far too light. As a generalisation they were made in four grades and stamped accordingly viz 1). W.E. Hill & Sons 2) W.E.H. & S. 3) H & S 4) Hill. Other stampings are known and many were unstamped as not coming up to standard yet being quite useful bows: those stamped W.E. Hill may have been made by James Tubbs when he first worked for W.E. Hill. In many bows the maker can be identified by marks or numbers on the silver or gold face, also after 1928 most bows were dated on the stick under the frog. During the seventies the firm moved to Great Missenden and ceased trading in 1990.

HILTON Thomas James b1868   *Gorleston*
He worked between about 1890 and 1930 and made about 50 quite good instruments mostly violins on the Strad pattern.

HINDS Frederick   *London*
He worked circa 1760 and made a few violins of good quality but his main production was viola de gambas, some of which have been converted into 'cellos.

HINTON J.   *London*
He was an amateur maker who worked c. 1835.

HIRCUTT   *London*
He worked c. 1600; his violins have a high arching and are primitive as might be expected from the date.

HISLOP John
Known only from a quite well made viola labelled No. 42 and dated 1880.

HOFMANN G.W.   *Dubliln*
He worked in Dublin during the first quarter 20th century and made some
really fine violins on the Strad model. He had an association with Gustav Meinel
since instruments are seen labelled "Meinel & Hoffman, Dublin". The firm was
still active in Dublin in 1958.

HODDINOTT J.   *Wimborne*
He was a wealthy amateur who made violins, violas and 'cellos during the
second quarter of the 20th century. They are quite well made. Many were
given away by him to local players.

HOLDEN David W.   *Mankinholes Todmorden*
He was an amateur maker and repairer. His work is satifactory but decidedly on
the heavy side. One 'cello dated 1960 was well made but very weighty with
thick edges, nicely varnished with a pale golden varnish and the tone was
good. He also made some tenor viols.

HOING Clifford A. 1903 - 1988   *High Wycombe*
He was a fine craftsman who was first a woodcarver. He worked at 137 West Wycombe
Road and made about 150 violins and violas and one 'cello - he also made a few bows.
The violins are styled after Guarnerius and the 'Messie' Strad and his violas principally
on an individual model which he referred to as the 'Diploma' viola and which has a
body length of 416mm: he held decided views on viola size and was totally against the
then popular 'Tertis' model. Some of the instruments he made were not labelled and
very skilfully faked to look old, they now probably bear suitable Italian labels. He retired
from making about 1971 but continued to carry out restorations for a few years.

HOLDER Thomas Jacques 1842 - 1922   *London & Blackheath*
His work is seldom labelled but sometimes he used the pseudonym Tomasso
Giacomo Auldero. His work is excellent in every respect, it is a pity that so little
of it is recognisable.

HOLDER Ernest L. b1878   *Blackheath*
He was the brother of Thomas and worked from about 1900 to 1950 producing
some remarkably fine instruments which are rather on the heavy side. Label
"E.L. Holder/Violin Maker and Repairer/125, Lee Road, Blackheath, S.E. 23".

HOLDER Thomas James b1874
Brother of Ernest L. but worked only for a short while in England before setting
up in business in Paris.

HOLE A.P. c. 1870   *Leicester*

HOLLARD George 1814 - 1894   *Compton Dundon*
He made a few rustic violins and carried out local repairs.

HOLLOWAY John   *London*
He worked between about 1775 and 1795 at 31 Gerrard Street but his work is
not particularly good.

HOLMES Henry   *Leeds & Halifax*
He worked at these places between about 1910 and 1920.

HOLMES Stanley b1879   *Liverpool*
He was a self taught amateur who achieved very successful results. His violins are on the Strad model with a flattish arching, sharply raised edgework and corners, well cut soundholes, neatly finished and well varnished. He worked from about 1905 to 1930.

HONE P.A.   *Coventry*
He worked from about 1900 to 1950 as a maker and repairer. His output of new instruments was fairly small but they are well made if a shade on the heavy side.

HOOTON b1873   *Ashton in Makerfield*
An amateur maker; his work is only of average quality.

HOPKINS E. b1915   *Portsmouth*
He was taught violin making by A.E. Harfield (q.v.) and made a number of violins as an amateur on the Strad model; these are well made and finished with a golden brown oil varnish.

HOPKINS   *Worcester*
He worked circa 1860 but not very well.

HORRIDGE Walter b1875   *Stamford*
He was taught violin making by A. Scholes of Rushden and, being a woodcarver, soon overcame any technical problems so that his violins are of good workmanship and attractive.

HOSKINS James   *Camerton*
He made violins, violas and 'cellos and his work is reasonably good.

HOWELL P.   *Exeter*
It is not known whether or not he was a maker. His trade card refers to "instruments improved and repaired". He worked during the first quarter of the 19th century.

HOWARD Frank 1868 - 1930   *Nottingham & London*
He commenced as a professional maker in 1894 having previously been making violins as an amateur while working at his trade as a cabinet maker. He was responsible for teaching very many pupils violin making at his classes held at the Northern Polytechnic. He made about 100 violins as well as a few violas and 'cellos. The workmanship is good, purfling rather broad, edges and corners strong yet neatly finished and the scroll well carved. The varnish is rather 'hard' looking and often a golden brown shade. He also made a few bows.

HOWARTH H.   *Bury*
He was a professional violinist who made a few quite good violins circa 1920.

HOWSON A.T.   *London*
He was taught violin making by C. Fivaz and worked during the last quarter of the 19th century. His violins are on the Strad pattern, they are well made and covered with a red/brown oil varnish, which is put on rather thickly.

HOYLE Edward   *Todmorden*
He worked circa 1880. His violins are reasonably well made and covered with dark red varnish. He also made some of eccentric pattern.

HUDSON George 1859 - 1916   *Skegness*
He commenced making instruments about 1885 and completed about 100 violins, violas and 'cellos and one double bass (dated 1889). Every instrument is numbered and dated. His work is good and the oil varnish particularly attractive often in a fine deep red shade. In addition to a label some are branded G. HUDSON below the button. He also was esteemed as a repairer. No. 17 dated 1887 and No. 71 dated 1901 gives some guide as to his making activity.

HUDSON George-Wulme 1862 - 1952   *London & Chessington*
He made his first instrument in 1897 and was still working into his 80's. The majority of his early work (apart from his first efforts) was devoted to making reproduction instruments and indeed he made these at various times throughout his working life. They sometimes have true Italian names and others have names invented by himself e.g. Pietro Marezzi, Gasparo Rovelli, Giacomo Ferrazi and, of course, the pseudonym he adopted Giovanni Caressi. There is no doubt that he was a fine craftsman, the materials he used for the backs and ribs are frequently very handsome, indeed some are pictures, and a very straight grained wood for the tables. In varnishing he was not always so successful since some of the early varnishes are beginning to craze. He made some violas but, unaccountably, these are clumsy and heavy: he made no 'cellos.

HUME Alexander b1941   *Dundee, Peterborough & London*
Originally a professional violinist and teacher he first took up violin making as a hobby but later became a professional maker. In every respect his work is of high quality even in his cheaper class of violins, and the materials always of good quality. The edges are rather heavily beaded. The fronts of some of his instruments seem to be made of a type of spruce very prone to split perhaps accentuated by the fact the plates are worked very thinly. The varnish is of good quality inclined to paleness and thinly laid on. He made violins, violas and 'cellos, also a few bows.

HUMPHREYS George b1859   *Timberland, Lincoln*

HURLEY Arthur   *Tondu*
He made violins as an amateur circa 1920.

IMRIE W.H.   *Edinburgh*
He was an amateur maker who worked c. 1920. While the workmanship is quite reasonable his instruments have too much wood in them for the tone to be satisfactory.

INGRAM David   *Edinburgh*
He worked during the first quarter 19th century but his efforts were not very good.

INGRAM Henry   *Durham*
He worked circa 1820 but made few instruments and those not very well.

INGRAM Walter *Bristol*
He worked circa 1830, his violins look nice but do not sound well.

INGRAM William b1869 *Linlithgow*
He was an amateur maker who made a number of violins on the Guarnerius model from about 1920 to 1930, they are well made and nicely varnished.

INVERARITY James b1862 *Aberdeen*
He made a large number of instruments of all types which are quite well made and varnished . Label "Jas. R. Inverarity/Aberdeen 1920".

IRESON Frank b1868 *Bishop Aukland*
He was an amateur maker whose violins are quite well made but frequently over long in the body; some are built on more conventional lines. His varnish is generally a light orange shade. Label "F.H. Ireson/Fecit/Newgate Street/Bishop Auckland".

IRVING George *London*
Known only by a well made violin having a bird's eye maple back labelled "Made by Geo. Irving/London/1914".

IRWIN E.J. b1875 *Bradford*
He was an amateur maker who achieved quite good results between the years 1900 and 1930. Label "Made by E.J. Irwin, Bradford 1922".

JACKLIN Cyril William 1902 - 1988 *London & Loughton*
He was one of the many pupils of Frank Howard. First he was in partnership with F. Ciesla but in 1927 left to work on his own account in Robert Street, Regents Park. He moved to Shaftesbury Avenue in 1931 and was 'bombed out' in 1940 so worked from his home in Loughton until 1949 when he became a director of Albert Arnold; on the firm closing in 1956 he returned to Loughton. He made relatively few instruments, the violins are mostly on the Guarnerius model and number about eighteen, he also made a few violas and one 'cello. All of these are well made. He was a good restorer and an acknowledged expert on old instruments.

JACKLIN T. 1838 - 1917 *Hull*
No relationship to the foregoing. He worked at Hull during the period 1880 - 1910 and his work is very good. Label "Thos. Jacklin/16 Ocean Place/Hull 1891". His violins are on the Strad model using good materials and covered with a rich golden brown oil varnish.

JAMES Raymond Frank *Whitchurch*
He advertised himself as a maker and repairer during the period 1955 - 1965 but I have seen no example of his work.

JAMES Rhys P. b1909 *Bridgend*
He was taught violin making by G. Schliepps an Estonian maker living in Bridgend. He took charge of the Remploy workshop where violins were made for a while and later worked on repairs at which he became very adept. He made few instruments.

JAMES Stephen *Bristol*
He worked circa 1820 making violins on the Amati model quite well.

J'ANSON Edward Popplewell   *Leeds & Manchester*
He was a pupil of William Booth Junior and worked between about 1840 and
1875. He was a much better maker than his teacher mainly making violins but a
few violas and 'cellos are known. Much of his work is unlabelled (or the labels
have been removed). He was, from the evidence of a label working in Leeds in
1854 and by 1872 was in Manchester. His work is first class.

JAMIESON Thomas   *Aberdeen*
He worked circa 1830 - 1845 probably an amateur maker whose work is of
average quality.

JAY Henry   *London*
He worked from 1740 - 1770. He made some quite attractive violins rather
highly arched and having a sweet small tone. The 'cellos are under 735mm
body length rather fully arched and excellent tonally but not powerful. The
varnish is sometimes a deep red/brown and at others shades of golden brown.
Label "Made by Henry Jay/in Long Acre, London, 1748".

JEFFERY John 1841 - 1918   *Chirnside*
He was an amateur maker who made about 50 violins in various classical
models. The backs and ribs are of handsome wood, the workmanship excellent
in every detail and the varnishing splendidly carried out using a fine oil varnish
of red/brown or golden brown shades.

JENKENSON John   *Portsmouth*
He worked at 119 London Road, Portsmouth. The workmanship in his
instruments is good and he used good materials. The edges are left rather flat
but nicely rounded and the purfling faultlessly inlaid. He favoured a golden
brown varnish and this is rather thinly applied. Printed label "John
Jenkenson/Violin Maker and Restorer/119 London Road, Portsmouth 1907".

JENKINS Thomas b.1819   *Haverfordwest*
He worked circa 1830 - 1845 probably an amateur maker whose work is of
average quality.

JERMY Arthur b.1867   *Hackney, London*
He was a professional maker and repairer who worked at 6 Crossway,
Kingsland, Hackney between about 1895 and 1920. His violins are well made
but there are few of them since his time was taken up with repairing.

JERVIS Frank   *Belfast*
He worked circa 1800 and made some good violins on the Amati pattern.

JOHNSON A.W.   *London*
He was a bowmaker who worked for Hill's.

JOHNSON John   *London*
He worked between about 1750 and 1770. His violins are somewhat on Stainer lines
but the model is larger and the arching reduced (but it is still high), soundholes set
straight and wide in the stem, the backs prettily flamed, the bellies of fine grain and
worked very thin so that they are often badly cracked, purfling near to the edge but
often it is replaced by ink lines. The varnish is thin in texture and most often golden

brown in colour. The tone is clear but piercing. On the whole his work is variable and while a few instruments are really good these are definitely in the minority. He also made some 'cellos in which the general characteristics of his violins are duplicated.

JOHNSON Joseph   *Backworth*
Known only by his label in a fairly well made violin "Joseph Johnson/Violin Maker/Backworth November 1900".

JOHNSON William A.   *Leicester*

JOHNSTON Thomas   *Edinburgh*
He was an amateur maker who worked circa 1910. His violins are on the Guarnerius style, quite well made and covered with a deep red varnish which has slightly crackled.

JOHNSTON James   *Pollockshields*
He worked circa 1880 as an amateur and his work is excellent

JOHNSTONE William b.1880   *Edinburgh*
His violins made in Strad and Guarnerius styles are excellent.

JONES David   *Merthyr Tydfil*
He worked circa 1800.

JONES John 1833-1906   *Port Dinorwic*
He was an amateur maker whose violins are not very well made but have a reputation for sounding well.

JONES W.R.   *Barnstaple*
He worked from about 1900-1940. His trade card informed his clients that he was "Maker and Teacher of the Violin-Repairer of all string instruments-Bows rehaired at short notice-35 years experience". Jan Hambourg praised his violins but the only ones I have seen were made from handsome wood and decidedly 'tubby', the workmanship not bad and the varnish - a red colour - passable. He worked at 59 Gloucester Road, Barnstaple.

JONES W.H. c.1950   *Tipton*

JUBB William   *Horsforth, Leeds*
He worked circa 1920 as a professional maker and repairer. His instruments are rather heavily built with strong edges, good workmanship and materials and covered with an oil varnish of butterscotch shade. He also made some exquisite miniature instruments.

JUDGE Michael b.1886   *Dublin*
He worked in Dublin during the first quarter of the 20th century. Whilst the workmanship is neat and satisfactory certain details are eccentric such as very wide purfling, long soundholes and an original outline. They are varnished shades of orange/brown.

JONES J.   *Wrexham*
He worked as an amateur circa 1900 using a large Strad pattern and with fairly good results.

KEEBLE Jowett F. b.1867   *Cirencester*
He made a number of violins and quite well too, but his absorbing interest was
experimenting with various varnishes to ascertain their effect on the tone of
the instrument. He arrived at the perfectly sound conclusion that once the
instrument has been properly regulated and the wood treated to preserve the
regulation 'in the white' then the coloured varnish (provided that its
formulation does not impair the vibrations) has no influence on the tone and its
function is entirely cosmetic.

KEENAN Edward b.1876   *Dublin*
He was a professional maker and repairer who worked at 5 Spenser Street,
North Strand, Dublin. He commenced making violins as a self taught amateur
and succeeding at this decided to become a professional. His violins are
principally on the Strad pattern but some are made on Guarnerius lines. The
workmanship is fine, strongly made might best describe it. Label "Made
by/Edward Keenan/Dublin Anno 1918" and signed.

KEEN W.   *London*
He worked around 1800 and the style of his work is similar to other London
makers of the period who made for the trade.

KELLEWAY A.E.   *Southampton*
He was probably an amateur maker but his work is good. He used the Strad
model for his violins and covered these with an oil varnish.

KELLY John   *Paisley*
He worked circa 1830 and made violins and 'cellos.

KELMAN James b.1824   *Aberchirder*
He was an amateur maker who started violin making late in life and made about
forty instruments on the Strad model. He used for most of his instruments a
printed label "Made by/James Kelman/Auchintoul, Banffshire/189*".

KENDLE Philip c.1820   *Hereford*

KENNEDY Alexander   *Wallsend on Tyne*
Label "A.Kennedy/Maker/Wallsend,19++".

KENNEDY Alexander 1695-1785   *London*
His violins are in the Stainer style but not so tubby as many English makers of
the period who base their works on the German master. They are neatly made
and purfled and covered with a thinly applied varnish. He made some 'cellos as
well and these are of flatter modelling. He made instruments for the trade and
many are unlabelled.

KENNEDY John 1730-1816   *London*
He was the nephew and pupil of Alexander and worked from about 1750. He
worked mainly for the trade but also left some signed violins, one of which,
dated 1754 is a handsome instrument covered with a good red/brown varnish.
He made no 'cellos.

KENNEDY Thomas 1784-1870 *London*
He was the son and pupil of John Kennedy and also taught by Thomas Powell. He worked at various addresses first in Princes Street, Westminster and then at Nassau Street and from 1816-1849 at 364 Oxford Street. He was a prolific maker said to have made over 2,000 instruments including more than 300 'cellos. Some of the violins are not at all good but there is no doubt that Thomas Kennedy was a most accomplished workman capable of producing the finest work; this does not necessarily mean the finest tone as many makers and players have discovered. Not only did he make personally signed instruments but he also worked for the trade and some of the 'cellos stamped GOULDING were his productions. His best works are made from handsome woods and many of them are based on the Amati model with excellent workmanship. In varnishing he was not always successful since many of his instruments have a very badly crazed varnish, the deep red ones in particular. The violas are good, a common size is 395mm, they are a bit squarish top and bottom and have long wide corners. Best are his 'cellos and some of these are exceptionaly fine mostly around 725mm body length but occasionally as long as 760mm, rather unusual at that period. The backs are often beautifully figured and the workmanship first class: despite this the tone is sometimes a disappointment when one has viewed the fabrication with admiration. He used various labels, sometimes no label but signed inside the back and at other times, particularly with 'cellos, signed under the tailgut.

KENYON Albert b.1895 *Bradford*
He worked chiefly on repairs but has made a few violins.

KERR Walter *Newcastle*
He worked c. 1900. He was an amateur maker who completed some good sounding instruments - violins, violas and 'cellos - of fairly good workmanship but in some cases the varnish he used has badly crazed.

KIRKWOOD Robert *Edinburgh*
He was an amateur maker c. 1870.

KIRKWOOD William b.1884 *Forfar*
He made a few good violins c. 1950 but is, perhaps, better known for his hand carved bridges and a soundpost setter of special design which grips the soundpost rather than impaling it.

KNIGHT F.R. b.1870 *Reigate*
He was an amateur maker who was taught violin making by W. Glenister. He made about 50 quite nice instruments, the violins being on the Strad pattern and varnished in various shades of brown.

KOHLER Ernest *Edinburgh*
His label is seen in and sometimes branded on violins but these have been made by others and they appear to be principally continental imports, some of them are rather nice.

KYLE David *Dalry*
His violins are labelled "David Kyle,Maker/Dalry 1859" as an example. The workmanship is reasonably competent, using figured woods, 359mm body, Strad style and covered with a golden brown varnish.

LACEY John Edward c.1925   *Felixstowe*

LAING James   *Penicuik*
He was an amateur maker who adopted the Strad model for his violins. His
workmanship is quite good and they are varnished golden brown. Label "James
Laing/Kirkhill/Penicuik 1919".

LAIDLAW J.W. b.1864   *Newcastle*
He worked circa 1920. His violins are on the Guarnerius pattern, quite well
made with strong edges and covered with an orange red varnish. The tone of
them is good.

LAIDLAW J.N.   *London*
He worked circa 1950 and before this was employed by Hill's.

LAING Alexander   *Dundee*
He worked from about 1915-1930. His violins are nicely made and varnished an
orange shade of golden brown.

LAMB John I b.1823   *Shiremoor*
He worked as an amateur from about 1860-1890. His work is not bad but not
particularly good either, neither is the varnishing. Label "Made by John
Lamb/Shiremoor 1886".

LAMB John II   *Shiremoor*
Son of the above and also an amateur maker who made about sixty instruments
which are slightly improved versions of his father's but heavy in construction
and with the plates left too thick which accounts for their sluggishness in tone.

LANCASTER Arthur Catton b.1869   *Colne*
A professional maker and repairer during the period about 1890 to 1925. His
violins follow Stradivarius and Guarnerius and are made of handsome woods
with good workmanship and excellently varnished.

LANE Ernest A.P.   *Canterbury & Brighton*
He was an amateur maker who worked between about 1920 and 1930. His
violins are quite well made on a large Strad model 363mm body length and
varnished golden brown. Label "Ernest A.P. Lane/1923 Brighton".

LANG J.S.   *Wandsworth*
He worked c. 1900 but his work is not very good and the model he worked on
overlong.

LANGONET Alfred Charles 1917-1975   *London & Rottingdean*
He was apprenticed to his father C.F. Langonet at Hill's. In 1946 he was in
business with his father in London. He continued this after the death of his
father, later retiring to Rottingdean. His output of instruments was not large
and in every respect they are first class. He was an esteemed restorer and
expert.

LANGONET Charles Francois 1861-1929   *London*
He worked for Hill's for 48 years.

LANGONET Charles Frank b.1888 *London & Rottingdean*
Son of the preceding. He worked for Hill's for 36 years, being for many years head of their restoration workshop.

LANT Ernest Francis b.1901 *Sevenoaks*
He was taught violin making by Biddulph and made violins, violas, 'cellos and several double basses: he also made a few bows. He was a prolific workman but his work is not the epitome of carefulness. The modelling is rather flat, generally nicely figured woods, often the scroll chamfers are blackened, the edges are flattish, purfling a bit shaky and the varnish thin in texture although adequately coloured. Label "Ernest Francis Lant/Violin Maker and Repairer/Flat 5, 15 St. John's Road/Sevenoaks/No. 307 1965". He was working still in 1969.

LAPWOOD Ronald E. b.1904 *London*
He commenced as a repairer but has made a few instruments of average merit.

LATTEN H.G. *Lewisham*
He worked c. 1925 and was taught by Frank Howard. As an amateur he made a number of carefully finished violins. Label "H.G. Latten/maker/Lewisham 1926".

LAUGHER William b.1830 *Redditch*
He was an amateur maker and completed about 60 violins and violas, these are very well made and nicely varnished.

LAURENCE –. c. 1935 *Worth Matravers*

LAWLEY A.E. *Burton-on-Trent*
He worked circa 1930 and was probably an amateur maker but from an example dated 1933 - a violin on a large Strad pattern, there is nothing amateur about his work. M/S label.

LAWRENCE Ronald c.1960 *Pontypridd*

LEADER James Henry *Bristol*
He worked about 1830.

LEAKE H. c.1820 *Huntley*

LEE H.W. *London & Blackheath*
He started making violins about 1920 having been taught at the Ministry of Works Music Trades Training Centre. He was a prolific maker of all four stringed instruments and his work is of good quality (No. 41 dated 1924).

LEE Percy 1871-1953 *Cricklewood, London*
He was a professional violist who made about 50 instruments, a large proportion of which were violas; he also made some fine viola d'amores. He learned violin making with Haynes and Co. of Gray's Inn Road. He had some collaboration with Richard Fox of Enfield (q.v.) and some instruments bear their joint names. His instruments are very finely made of choice materials and beautifully finished. Label "Percy Lee Fecit/London, 1917".

LEGGATT C. 1880-1917 *London*
A bowmaker who worked for Hill's.

LENTZ Jacob *London*
He made a quantity of double basses around the third quarter of the 18th century but few other instruments.

LENTZ Johann Nicholas *London*
He worked in Chelsea circa 1800. Much of his work is unlabelled and made for the trade, it is nothing much. His output included a few 'cellos and these are rather better but with a forbiddingly dark varnish.

LENTZ Johann Friedrich *London*
Son of the above who worked with his father and absorbed much of his style of work.

LEWER -. *London*
He worked c. 1760 in Moorfields. His violins are rather high built but not excessively so, the soundholes are short and upright, nicely raised edges, short narrow corners, backs too thin and tables too thick for satisfactory tone which is, in consequence, muffled. The varnish is a nice red/brown in colour. They are sometimes labelled, but not always.

LEWIS Edward *London*
He worked from about 1690-1740. His violins are frequently overlong in the body but some, more highly arched, are more conventional in this respect. All of the work is good and the varnishing, with a rich red/brown (sometimes a golden yellow) varnish skilfully done. He made violas and 'cellos as well as violins. Label "Edward Lewis/over against Earl's Court/in Drury Lane, London,1732".

LEWIS Thomas *Gloucestershire*
He worked circa 1920, probably an amateur although his label is a printed one. His work is good and clean but the varnish he used is rather opaque.

LIESSEM Remerus *London*
He worked from about 1730-1760. He must have come to work in London from the continent. His violins are small in size and highly arched but they are splendidly made; it is a pity that with such skill he did not use a better model. The same remark applies to the 'cellos he made: these are just under 735mm in body length, the backs nicely figured and everything about the workmanship good, the modelling results in a very noticeable flattish 'tableland" on which the bridge sits. The varnish is satisfactory and usually golden brown and slightly opaque. Label (written, apparently, on vellum "Remerus Liessem/London 1742".

LIGHT Edward *London*
His name turns up in violins around 1800 but he did not make these himself, they were supplied by contemporary 'trade' makers.

LIGHT George *Exeter*
He worked circa 1790. His violins are on the Amati style with the work nicely carried out and covered with a golden brown varnish. Label "George Light/Violin Maker near the Cathedral/Exeter 1785". Sometimes stamped G. LIGHT under the button.

LILLEY James   *Leeds*
He worked from about 1800-1820 and his work is of good quality.

LINDSAY David   *Edzell*
He was an amateur maker who worked circa 1900. He used a large model Strad pattern and his workmanship is quite satisfactory. Sometimes he used the Guarnerius pattern. The varnish he used is generally red/brown. Label "D.R.Lindsay/Edzell,N.B.".

LINDSAY Michael 1837-1906   *Stockton on Tees*
He might be classed as a self taught amateur maker but he later adopted violin making as a living. During the period 1860 to 1905 he made over 500 instruments of all four types. His violins are on the Strad pattern but some of them, fortunately not all, are well over the standard length. The workmanship is good but the thicknessing of the plates is faulty. his 'cellos in particular having far too much wood in them. The wood for the backs and ribs is generally nicely figured but the varnish is not up to the standard of the workmanship, it is generaly golden brown or reddish shades. Printed label "Michael Lindsay M+L /Maker/Stockton-on-Tees 1898".

LINDSAY W.H.   *Cardiff*
An amateur maker who worked c.1920.

LINDSEY David   *Gateshead*
Known only by a label in a well made violin, Strad style, nicely figured woods and covered with a golden brown varnish. Label "David Lindsey/Violin & Violin Bow Maker/Gateshead/Violins carefully repaired".

LIPMAN S. c.1930   *Manchester*

LISTER John   *Leeds*
He worked circa 1720. His violins are high in model following the English style of the Stainer pattern but his results were not good.

LOCK George Herbert b.1850   *Shrewsbury*
He was a schoolteacher who made about 60 violins and 3 'cellos of very fair workmanship. The violins are on a pattern akin to Stradivarius but differing in points of detail. On some of his instruments the varnish has started to crackle.

LOGAN John b.1844   *Abington, Lanarkshire*
He worked from about 1870 to 1898 as an amateur and made about 50 violins of good workmanship most of which are on the Guarnerius pattern. The backs are generally of handsome figure and the edges strongly raised but this not overdone. His printed label in a violin dated 1894 of handsome appearance and varnished red/brown reads "Made by/John Logan/Abington,N.B. 1894".

LOMAX Jacob b.1850   *Bolton*
He was a pawnbroker who worked from his shop at 11 Durham Street, Bolton. In addition to his normal work he made, repaired and dealt in violins etc. as a sideline. They are well made and varnished with a preparation which he made himself.

LONGMAN & BRODERIP   *London*
This firm put their name in or, more frequently, stamped it on to instruments supplied to them by other makers, one of whom was Benjamin Banks I. Violas stamped with their name are generally small and most probably were made by Joseph Hill.

LONGMAN & LUKEY   *London*
Much the same remarks apply as written for the previous name, in fact the former continued as Longman & Lukey. Various makers supplied instruments some of the better ones being made by Lockey Hill.

LONGSON F.H.   *Stockport*
He worked c. 1900 but his work is not very good.

LONG James   *Cork*
He was an amateur maker who worked c. 1925; his work is of good quality.

LONGVILLE G.H.   *Honor Oak*
He worked as an amateur circa 1930 using a typed label.

LOTT George Frederick 1780-1868   *London*
He was the eldest son of J.F. Lott I and was apprenticed to Davis in Coventry Street for whom he continued to work until 1847 when he opened his own shop on the corner of Princes (now Wardour) St. and Gerrard St. His instruments are skillful copies of Italian masters and the workmanship is fine.

LOTT John Frederick I 1775-1853   *London*
He came to London from Germany in 1795 and for some time worked for Dodd. Later he set up his own shop in King Street, Seven Dials. He made relatively few violins which are on the model of Stradivarius. His violas are good but too small at 387mm for true viola sonority but his Strad style 'cellos are really excellent. His fame rests with his double basses with the Italian style imitated. Label J.F.Lott/Maker/London".

LOTT John Frederick II 1805-1871   *London*
He was the second son of J.F. Lott I and his pupil. He worked with his father and was apprenticed to Davis (1820) remaining with him until 1852 by which time Edward Withers had taken over the Davis firm (in 1846). He opened his own shop at 60 Wardour Street in 1860. He is best known as a maker of fake old instruments showing all of the features of the originals and finished off with remarkable artificial ageing. His best violins are the Guarnerius 'copies' but sometimes he overdid the details and some of the features of the original are exaggerated especially in the soundholes which may be overlong. Violins in other styles were made but infrequently. The violas are larger than his father's, generally about 400mm, and these have a 'cello type heel to the pegbox, occasionally the style of the soundholes is not at all pretty with wide lower wings and a stiff look about them. The 'cellos are fine. On some instruments the varnish is chippy and on some it is hard and red but on most it has been so chopped about to give the appearance of age that it is not easy to determine what it might have been had the instruments been varnished normally. His instruments are seldom labelled and his name is a common attribution for any good instrument of the period which looks anything like a Guarnerius.

LOUDON James *Liverpool*
He worked c. 1880. His violins are large in body - 362mm - and, allegedly copies of Guarnerius. Label "Joseph Guarnerius fecit Cremone anno 1718/James Loudon, Violin Maker/Liverpool, October 1876".

LOW W.F. *Sunderland*
He was probably an amateur maker working c. 1890; his work is fairly good.

LOWE John *Glasgow*
Known only by a 'cello labelled "Made by John Lowe/no. 2. Glasgow 1926".

LUFF William 1904-1993 *London & Worthing*
He was one of this century's leading makers. He commenced his interest in violin making by becoming a pupil of Frank Howard as so many makers did, and his ability was so great that he was offered employment with Dykes and Son as a restorer, while here he was greatly influenced by Roger and Max Millant. He stayed with Dykes for eleven years and then from 1932 set up a workshop at his home. From 1939 to 1946 he was working on electronics for the RAF but as soon as he was released joined J & A Beare with whom he stayed for nine years. In 1955 he set up his own shop in Shepherd's Bush where he remained until his 'retirement' in 1969 to near Worthing. Here he continued to make instruments. His violins are on various models but he principally favoured that of Guarnerius del Gesu. As one might expect the workmanship and materials were first class and his instruments were praised for their fine tone; his success did much to dispel the myth that violins have to be old to sound well. Mostly the finish of his instruments is to give the appearance of age but this is never overdone as is the case with many French copyists. He made about 260 violins, 40 violas and 1 'cello.

LUDBROOK William c.1925 *Leeds*

LUNDIE William c.1780 *Aberdeen*

LUTON George *Leicester*
Probably an amateur maker who worked c. 1850; his work is fair.

LYALL John *Edinburgh*
He worked circa 1895 and his work is very fair.

LYE Henry *Camerton*
He was a carpenter and amateur maker who was probably taught by John White. He was employed on the Camerton Court Estate and during his long working life from about 1860-1920 he made many violins, violas and 'cellos. The work is variable, the best being just short of good but he also made some violins which were rather bulgy and covered with a red varnish resembling paint. His best violins are after, but not strict copies of, Guarnerius. The 'cellos are rather on the small side and some essential dimensions inaccurate. His best varnish is an oil one in shades of orange brown or red brown. He used both handwritten labels and one printed in Old English lettering.

LYONS James d.1938 *Burscough*
He was a cabinet maker by trade and made violins, violas, 'cellos and double basses as a hobby. They are well made and nicely varnished generally in a light golden brown colour.

McCARTER John *Dalkeith*
He was an amateur maker who, in the period about 1920-1955, made a number of good instruments generally on a large Guarnerius style.

McCARTNEY James d.1924 *Mauchline*
He was a blacksmith by trade. His violins are roughly made and poorly finished.

McCRINDLE John *Glasgow*
An amateur maker circa 1890 whose work is only fair.

McDONNELL Alexander *Dublin*
Known only by a label in a viola of 390mm body length made from plain woods and varnished golden brown "Made by Chaz and Alexander McDonnell/Dublin 1777" and branded below the button.

MACDONALD C. *Hull*
He made violins and bows.

McDOUGALL A *Eastbourne*
An amateur maker who commenced making in 1939.

MACE B.T. *Bexley Heath*

MACGEORGE d.1821 *Edinburgh*
He worked for some time with Matthew Hardie and later on his own. His violins are very similar to Hardie's not only in the model and style but also in the tone which is clear but rather hard. The varnish is different being of a light reddish colour. His instruments are mostly unlabelled but have "G.M'George Edinburgh" written inside

McGILL William *Edinburgh*
His label reads 'William McGill/Maker/Ednr. Jun 1810" and branded McGill under the button. His work is of fair quality using faintly figured woods and having ink lines instead of purfling.

MacGILL James Campbell *Arran*
He made over 50 instruments including 3 'cellos and the work is good. Early instruments are spirit varnished but he soon changed to an oil varnish. He used no label but marked the inside of the back "J.C.M'Gill/Maker/Arran 189-".

McGREGOR A. *Edinburgh*
His work is very good, the backs and ribs of handsomely figured wood and covered with a good oil varnish red/brown or golden brown in colour.

M'INTOSH James 1801-1873 *Blairgowrie*
He was probably taught violin making by Peter Hardie. His early instruments are highly arched and narrow, generally one piece backs and with 'ink line' purfling, they are well made. Later ones are near to the Strad model, purfled and frequently made of handsome wood for the backs and sides. He made 204 violins, 10 violas and 35 'cellos and used a printed label "James M'Intosh/ Violin Maker, Blairgowrie/April 1861".

M'INTOSH John c.1920 *Edinburgh*

MACINTOSH John   *Galston*
He worked between about 1880-1926 and made some 60 violins. The early specimens are not at all good but he improved as he went on and later specimens varnished a pale orange colour are not at all bad. His name and other details are written inside the back.

McINTOSH John   *Dublin*
His violins are highly arched and the model small, quite well made and the varnish an orange brown colour. Label "John McIntosh/No.4 —Quay/Dublin 1815".

M'Kenzie Malcolm 1828-1904   *Dumbarton*
He was a prolific maker and his workmanship, while not being particularly refined, is not too bad either. Label "Malcolm M'Kenzie/Dumbarton".

MacIntosh William b.1852   *Dundee*
He worked from about 1892 to 1915 modelling his violins after Stradivarius and making them quite satisfactorily. Label "Made by/William M'Intosh/Dundee.

MACKIE Adam b.1871   *Aberdeen*
He was a cabinet maker who was taught violin making by James Gorrie. He worked in Aberdeen for six year until 1899 before emigrating. He did not label his violins while working in Scotland.

MacINTOSH John   *Galston*
He worked at Strath Cottage, Galston around the turn of the century and made some quite good violins, some of which were decorated.

MacINTOSH John   *Dublin*
He was a pupil of Thomas Perry and succeeded to his business. His work is rather variable from quite common violins with no purfling to reasonably well made Strad style instruments - presumably he made (or had made for him) violins for different purses. Sometimes they are labelled and others are stamped MACKINTOSH on the back and/or by the tailpin.

McCLEAN E.P.   *Dover*
An amateur maker c. 1920 who produced some poor quality violins.

M'LAY William 1815- about 1885   *Crosshill, Kincardine on Forth*
He made about 50 violins, 6 violas and 6 'cellos but the workmanship is not good and they do not sound well. The name and address is written inside the back.

Mac LEOD D. c.1920   *Renfrew*

M'NEILL John 1850-1923   *Edinburgh & Dublin*
He was a professional violinist and a good maker. Taught by his father William M'Neill he worked first at Edinburgh and later in Dublin. His violins are on the Guarnerius model.

M'NEILL Thomas d.1917   *Dublin*
He worked at 140 Capel Street, Dublin with his brother John.

M'NEILL William b.1827 *Edinburgh*
His rather well made violins are on a sort of Guarnerius model but more highly arched, the wood for the backs is generally fairly plain and they are finished with an oil varnish dark amber in colour. He also made a few 'cellos.

MACPHAID John c.1870 *Monzie*

MACPHERSON A. c.1900 *Crieff*

McSWAN John *Partick*
He was an amateur maker who made about 80 violins of average merit between about 1880 and 1920.

MAGHIE J.F. *Dalston, Cumberland*
He worked circa 1900. His violins are on a large Strad model and while they are fairly well made and finished, the tone is loud and coarse. Label "John Fisher Maghie/at Dalston in Cumberland/fecit —".

MAHONEY Frederick Daniel b.1880 *London & Lavenham*
He worked for both F.W. Chanot and Joseph Chanot and made under his own label a considerable number of good instruments both in London and, after 1950, in Lavenham. A number of these are violas made to an original design.

MALCOLM F. c.1928 *Richmond*

MALLAS Alexander 1826-1891 *Leith*
He was a millwright by trade. As an amateur he made violins, violas and 'cellos which are of good workmanship and covered with a golden brown oil varnish. His instruments are on the heavy side and rather 'woody' in tone. Label, printed in Old English characters "A.Mallas/Maker/Leith 18—".

MALLINSON J. *Liverpool*
A label in a violin read "J.Mallinson/Manufacturer and repairer of Musical Instruments/19 Shaw's Brow, Liverpool". Nothing more is known of this person who may or may not have been a maker.

MANDER Harry *Hasder*
Known only by a label in a 'cello of 735mm body length, made from plain woods, fairly well made and purfled and varnished golden brown. Label "Made by/Harry Mander/Hasder/1807".

MANN John Alexander 1810-1889 *Glasgow*
He worked at Argyle Street from about 1845-1880. His work right from the start was good, choosing the Strad model and using choice materials. The varnishing is not to everyone's taste, being rather pale and made darker under the bridge like some of the cheap French workshop productions. It is said that he bought some violins 'in the white' from French makers, touched them up, varnished them and sold them as his own work. Label "Fair par/John A. Mann/Glasgow 1885".

MANN Thomas Howell *Cardiff and Bedford*
He was a Civil Engineer by profession and made a number of good violins between the years about 1905 and 1955. The early ones were made in Cardiff

up to about 1909. The work is always very clean and precise, the edges sharp and nicely rounded, soundholes excellently cut, scroll first class and purfling inlaid without any fault. The tone is powerful and of good quality. He never seemed to overcome problems with varnish which, though of pleasing colours, has in a number of instances begun to craze. Label in M/S "Thomas Howell Mann made me/Bedford 1911".

MANUEL Evan c.1820 *Merthyr Tydfil*

MARLAND John 19th century *Hurst*

MARNIE James *Pandanaram*
He was an amateur maker and taught by Findlay of the same town. He made about 40 violins on the Guarnerius model but rather roughly.

MARR W. *Newcastle*
He worked c. 1815, his violins being on the Amati model and very pleasingly made.

MARSHALL Arthur *Salford*
He worked circa 1920 with good workmanship and generally varnishing his violins red. He used a written label.

MARTIN John c.1870 *Gateshead*

MARTIN A. *London*
He worked c. 1790 at Hermitage Bridge, Wapping. His violins are of small body and have a medium/full arching, quite prominent edges, soundholes set upright and having more than the usual width between the top circles, brownish shades of varnish, the centre strip of purfling is very light in colour. His usual label gives Hermitage Bridge but another has been seen "A. Martin/Musical Instrument Maker/Near Kings Brook St./St. Katherines, London" also branded MARTIN below the button.

MARTIN Henry *Nottingham*
He worked c. 1800. His violins are very highly arched but quite well made.

MASOM George *London*
A little known maker who worked c. 1925. His work is very fine indeed. He either made for or was associated in some way with the "British Violin Makers Guild". He seemed to like making his violins with one piece backs and following the Guarnerius pattern.

MASTERS J.K.S. *Worthing*
He worked c. 1890. He made few violins but these are well made.

MASTERS J.W. c.1924 *Manningham*

MATHER Alexander b.1852 *Plumstead*
He worked as an amateur c. 1900.

MATTHEWS R.S. 1905-1979 *Croxley Green & Chorley Wood*
He was taught violin making by William Glenister and, as an amateur, made a fair number of well made violins and violas between about 1930 and 1970.

MAUCOTEL Charles 1807-1860 *London*
He came to London to work for Davis in 1844 and stayed on when Edward Withers took over, leaving in 1848 to set up his own business at 8 Rupert Street. All features of his work put this into the top class. Label "C.Maucotel/ Violin & Violoncello Maker/8 Rupert Street, Haymarket, London". He returned to France in 1860 and died there soon afterwards.

MAUNDER M.E. *London*
He was an amateur maker and his work is distinctly slipshod. No. 35 dated 1923.

MAWBY Frederick H. *Nottingham*
He made few instruments but these are nicely made, generally with one piece backs and covered with a dark golden brown varnish. Label "Frederick H. Mawby Maker/Nottingham 1920. F.H.M. No. 7".

MAXWELL Edwin *Wimbledon*
He worked circa 1920. An amateur maker, his work is fairly good. No. 19 dated 1940.

MAY -. *London*
He worked c. 1750 and built highly arched violins and violas which are well made.

MAYSON Stansfield *Manchester*
The son of Walter. His work is good but seldom seen. He worked from about 1895-1920.

MAYSON Walter H. 1835-1904 *Manchester & Newby Bridge*
A prolific maker who made 763 violins, 27 violas and 21 'cellos. Not all of the instruments are good, indeed many were obviously made quickly for a cheap sale, but the best are very well made (although not everyone would favour the original model on which many of the violins were made). He was self taught and made his first violin in 1873, the early instruments are conventional but he later adopted a model which is 364mm body length and broad as well. In his better instruments the wood is well figured, indeed some are very handsome, the edgework strong and well finished, soundholes well cut, excellent scroll carving and covered with a soft golden brown or reddish brown oil varnish. Many instruments have names given to them. The violas are 405mm body length or thereabouts and, like his 'cellos, are rather on the heavy side.

MEAD L. J. d. about 1958 *Cosham*
He was an amateur maker who made violins, violas and 'cellos of good workmanship and which sound well.

MEARES Richard *London*
He made a few violins and violas working about 1700. The violins are of medium arching, have short straight soundholes and a deep groove round the edge into which the purfling is inserted. The varnish is red brown and the tone small. Most of his output was lutes and violas. His son, also Richard, made a few violins.

MEESON Richard   *Islington*
It is not known if he was a maker. He was the inventor, with a Dr. Stones, of an elliptic tension bar. He worked from 14 Colebrook Row, Islington about 1870.

MEEK James b.1862   *Carlisle & Birkenhead*
He made about 80 violins, several violas and at least one 'cello. His work is excellent and covered with a good oil varnish of a deep red or orange brown shade.

MEEK William   *Carlisle*
He worked circa 1900 and was probably a son of the above. His work is very similar.

MEGGISON Alfred   *Manchester*
He worked c. 1800 and made some highly arched violins of little merit.

MEIKLE Robert 1817-1897   *Lesmahagow*
He was a violinist who made a number of well made violins.

MEINEL Gustav   *London & Dublin*
He worked first at 151/3 Wardour St., then moved to Hallam Street and finally to Dublin. His work is very good. Label "Gustav Meinel/Maker and Repairer/151 & 153 Wardour Street/London, W. 1897".

MELLON H.E. c.1924   *Redruth*

MENTIPLY Andrew b.1858   *Ladybank, Fife*
He was an amateur maker and self taught. He made about 60 violins and the work is good with individual touches; they are mostly on a conventional pattern but some have an overlong body length. The oil varnish was his own preparation and it was not very good. He also made a few bows.

MENZIES John   *Falkirk*
He worked c. 1830. His violins are rather too big in the body with deepish ribs using plain woods not too well put together. They are varnished dark brown and are not very desirable items.

MEREDITH L.   *London*
He worked c. 1735. His violins have certain resemblance to the Maggini style.

MERLIN Joseph   *London*
He worked in London c. 1770-1780. His violins are built on the Stainer pattern but not so highly arched, he generally used well figured wood for the backs and ribs and the workmanship is good but he failed to get a good tone.

MEYNELL A.R.   *London*
He worked for Charles Boullangier and took over his shop in Frith Street. He was not heard of after 1914.

MIGGE Otto   *London & Eastbourne*
Excellent workmanship often on overlarge models. Sometimes he put 'decorative' purfling designs on the back. Generally a sombre dark brown varnish.

MILES Frank *Brighton*
A woodwork teacher and amateur maker who produced some nice work.

MILES George d.1912 *Erith*
He made about 85 instruments. Early examples are rather insignificant, poor choice of wood and the workmanship not too good but in later ones he improved although following a rather large Stradivarius pattern. Label "Made by/George Miles/No. 74 Erith 1908".

MILES Ralf *Forest of Dean & Stroud*
Amateur maker whose instruments are good. He worked first in Royal Forest of Dean and later at Stroud from about 1957 onwards. Made violins, violas and 'cellos.

MILLER C. c.1880 *Tottenham*

MILLER John b.1861 *Dundee*
He made about 40 instruments as an amateur maker, these are on the Strad model covered with a reddish varnish and are attractive.

MILLHOUSE J. c.1890 *Nottingham*

MILLINGTON Ernest *Derby*
He worked c. 1928 as an amateur maker. He was employed by the L.M.S. Rly. Co. as a chemist and made a few instruments of good workmanship but is better known for an oil varnish which he formulated and which he sold to other makers: although quite good it had a tendency to craze.

MILNE Patrick Gordon b.1873 d.1949 *Glasgow & Aberdeen*
He worked from 1898 to 1920 in Aberdeen then moved to Glasgow. His violins are on the Guarnerius and Stradivarius models, the early ones spirit varnished and the later ones oil varnished. The work is rather variable but never bad, in fact the best ones are very good. He made about 70 violins as well as some violas and 'cellos. The woods are generally well figured and the varnish dark red or deep red/brown.

MILNE Peter b.1835 d.1912 *Aberdeen*
Father of Patrick. He was an amateur maker and made few instruments.

MILNER Frank *Sheffield*
A Violinist and Conductor who made some attractive instruments c. 1930. He (or a descendant) had a violin shop in Sheffield in 1958.

MILLER William *Maisey Newton*
He worked c. 1826 and was probably a local carpenter who made a few instruments including a 'cello. This was unpurfled, made from plain woods, rather rough, dark red/brown varnish. It made a very good sound.

MILTON Louis Frank 1898-1947 *Bedford*
He was a pupil of Scholes and worked from about 1920 until his early death. His violins are well made instruments modelled after Jos. Guarnerius using good materials and varnished golden orange or red brown. A 'cello however

was decidedly heavy in style with a wide overlap at the edges, thick uneven corners and a rather muddy varnish. His work was factored by Hawkes & Co. Label "Louis F. Milton/Bedford.England/No. 25 1924".

MINER D. B. c.1920   *Dunfermline*

MINSHULL Ernest Frederick b.1877   *Manchester & Leeds*
He worked for G.A. Chanot for fifteen years then on his own account in Leeds. His work using conventional Cremonese models is good.

MITCHELL George b.1823 d.1897   *Edzell*
His early instruments are rather highly arched but he later corrected this. Altogether he made over 100 instruments and these are of, excepting the early ones, good workmanship. They are not always labelled but the name etc. is written inside the back.

MITCHELL John c.1910   *Dunfermline*

MOFFATT J.W.   *London*
He worked c. 1860 and made violins and 'cellos of good workmanship. Not all instruments bearing his label were made by him since he sometimes imported German instruments into which he inserted his own label. Not always labelled but stamped under the button "J.W. MOFFATT/LONDON".

MONCKTON John E.   *Bredon, Wolverhampton*
He was an amateur maker who had some original ideas on violin construction and made a number of them around 1870.

MONK John King b.1846   *Lewisham & Merton*
He made over 250 instruments which are rather ordinary in quality, some have a triple bass bar system which he invented. Label (printed) "J.K. Monk/Maker/Merton, Surrey, S.W./No. 178 1908".

MOODY G.T.   *Southampton*
No. 8 dated 1916. A nicely made instrument bearing a printed label.

MOORE Alfred   *Isle of Man*
Excellent work; he made violins, violas and 'cellos and worked from about 1890 to 1910.

MOORE Anthony John b.1852   *Sunderland*
He was an artist and an amateur violin maker. He made few instruments (No. 20 is dated 1906 and his first one was made in 1886), but these are quite well made.

MOORE J.G. c. 1910   *Liverpool*
Fairly good work using rather plain woods, unlabelled but the name etc. inscribed on the inner back. deep red brown varnish.

MORGAN James 1839-1906   *Edinburgh*
He made about 20 violins and some 'cellos. The early ones were made at Kinkardine and are spirit varnished, later ones from Edinburgh are superior and oil varnished. Some are labelled while some just have the name written inside the back - "James Morgan/1895".

MORGAN William 1844-1922　　　　　　　　　　　*Dunottar Castle*
He made over 100 instruments which are not of refined workmanship but this quite satisfactory, the tone is however good.

MORRIS J. 19th century　　　　　　　　　　　　　　　　　*Bath*

MORRIS W. Meredith
Known best for his book British Violin Makers which went to two editions but he also made a few instruments and one, dated 1904, was good. Label "Guliemus Mereditus Morrisius/Garthensis/Faciebat Anno 1904".

MORRIS Henry　　　　　　　　　　　　　　　　　　*Darlington*
He was an amateur maker who made a dozen Guarnerius copies. They are well made and varnished golden yellow.

MORRISON Archibald 1820-1895　　　　　　　　　　*Glasgow*
He worked from 1840 as an amateur maker and for John Mann from 1860 to 1865 when he set up his own workshop as a professional maker. His violins are generally over long, commonly 362mm, on a sort of Stradivarius style.

MORRISON James b.1827　　　　　　　　　　　*Dunfermline*
Made about 40 violins on the Stradivarius model. The backs etc. are of figured wood and the tables of broad grained red pine. The varnish is a red oil preparation.

MORRISON John 1760-1827　　　　　　　　　　　　*London*
He worked in Princes St. Soho, moving to Shadwell in 1819 and later to Little Turnstile, Holborn. He worked mainly for the trade but some work is individually labelled, of these the 'cellos are the best. Label "Jn.MORRISON/Maker/44 Princes Street, Soho/London 1828".

MORTIMER J.W.　　　　　　　　　　　　　　　　　　*Cardiff*
He made violins, violas and 'cellos but the principal instrument for which he achieved a reputation was the double bass. His violins are often over long and the workmanship very satisfactory. Label "Made by/John W. Mortimer/Cardiff 1918". The varnish is an oil one and often orange brown in colour.

MOVERLEY Frederick　　　　　　　　　　*Stourport on Severn*
He was an amateur maker c. 1950. He made violins and violas (Tertis pattern) and these are of fair workmanship.

MOWBRAY David b.1868　　　　　　　　　　　　　　*Leith*
He commenced making about 1910 on the Stradivarius and Guarnerius models but was mainly occupied with repairs.

MOYA Hildago d.1927　　　　　　　　　　　　　*Leicester*
He was Mirecourt trained. He made violins on both Stradivarius and Guarnerius models and the work is in every respect the epitome of neatness. His instruments are covered with an oil varnish applied in a manner which is different from usual. He worked until 1920.

MUMBY Ernest b.1888　　　　　　　　　　　　　*Tottenham*
He was a pupil of Whitmarsh. His work is excellent using nicely figured woods and well finished. Label "Ernest Mumby/London 1937".

MUNRO William   *Dunfermline*
He was an amateur maker who worked c.1870. He used a peculiar model for
his violins and badly varnished them.

MURDOCH Alexander 1815-1891   *Aberdeen*
He made a great many violins only a few of which have any pretension to good
workmanship. Much of his large output is unlabelled, others are stamped
MURDOCH/ABERDEEN under the button.

MURDY Thomas   *Embleton*
Known only from a nicely made violin 14" body, very strongly raised edges,
nicely figured woods, covered with a thin red varnish and labelled "Made
by/Thomas Murdy 1888/EMBLETON". Also stamped THOS. MURDY under the
button. Obviously not the first violin he had made.

MURPHY Bartholomew c.1800   *Cork*

MURPHY Denis c.1830   *Dublin*

MURPHY John c.1830   *Cork*

MURRAY Alexander   *Morpeth*
He made a number of well made violins circa 1850.

MURRAY Daniel C. b. 1850   *Edinburgh*
He made over 50 violins and a few violas. The violins are generally on the
Guarnerius pattern but larger and varnished yellow or dark brown. The 'label'
is stamped with a rubber stamp on the top block and the back "DANIEL
MURRAY/Violin Maker/Edinburgh".

MURRAY David b.1850   *Gorebridge*
He made about 50 violins of Stradivarius and Guarnerius modelling working
from about 1880 to 1910. Not always the prettiest of materials used and the
instruments are often large in the body but the work is good. He generally
varnished red or shades of red.

MURRAY James b.1857   *Milldamhead, Dumfries*
An amateur maker whose instruments follow firstly Hardie's and, later,
Stradivarius. Yellow oil varnish which is not of good quality.

MURRAY John Brown b.1849   *Clarebrand*
His violins are made on the Stradivarius model with rather raised edges. The
work overall is above average and the instruments are well finished and nicely
varnished. M/S label "J.B. MURRAY/Clarebrand/18–".

MUST Frederick   *Shrewsbury*
An amateur maker c. 1800. He worked on the Amati model but the arching is
too full.

MUTTEN A.   *London*
He worked c.1900. His work is of average ability and he used a dark red varnish
applied rather thickly and patchily.

MYLES Francis c.1840   *Cardiff*

NAISBY Thomas H.   *Sunderland*
Worked c.1915. His work is of an excellent standard. He made violins and violas.

NANCE William Edwin b.1837   *Penarth*
An amateur maker who made about 100 violins many of which were of
eccentric design.

NANKIVELL Joseph   *Sunderland*
See under T. Carter-Walker.

NAPIER F. b.1884
Son of William. Apprenticed to Hill's as a bowmaker and worked with them for
a short time before giving up the craft.

NAPIER W. 1848-1932
A bowmaker who worked for Hill's. He also made a few quite good violins
following details given in Heron Allen's book.

NASH Thomas   *Ayr*
Amateur maker c.1900.

NAYLOR Isaac   *Leeds*
He was a pupil of Richard Duke. His work is very pleasing yet seldom seen. The
violins are on the Amati pattern and covered with a good golden brown varnish.

NELSON George c.1900.   *North Seaton, Northumberland*
Very good work.

NELSON George   *Clacton*
Amateur maker, not very productive.

NELSON James   *Glasgow*
An amateur maker working c.1890. His model is large, and the workmanship
not very good. He used an oil varnish, light orange in colour.

NEMES Stefan W. b.1908   *London & Kingston on Thames*
He made many violins, violas and 'cellos. The violins are on the Stradivarius and
Guarnerius models and are made with great care. Fine woods are used and the
insruments are covered with an excellent varnish. Label "S.W.NEMES/Violin
Maker/London Op.72 1980".

NEWCOMBE George 19th century   *Leicester*

NEWTON Isaac   *London*
He worked from about 1782 to 1820 but his work is not very good. It is seldom
labelled since he worked much for music shops.

NEWTON K.E.   *Holt*
An amateur maker who used propolis as an undercoat. He worked c.1960.

NEWTON Thomas   *London*
He worked c.1740. Not particularly good work covered with a poor varnish.

NICOL Thomas b.1840-1910   *Glasterlaw*
A violinist who made about 80 violins of good workmanship, mostly oil
varnished and sounding well. Label "T. NICOL/18Maker98/Glasterlaw".

NICOLL –. c.1920   *Montrose*

NICHOLSON James c.1780   *Stirling*

NISBET William 1828-1903   *Lint Mill*
A self taught amateur who made a large number of violins on a sort of Amati
style with wide purfling, rather wide corners, well carved scroll with eyes
prominent, generally one piece figured backs, belly wood of strong grain and
covered with reddish shades of varnish. No label but "Wm.NISBET/Lint
Mill/1886" inscribed with a pencil where the label would normally be placed.

NISHAN Ernest c.1895   *Manchester*

NOBLE Hugh b.1849   *Dundee*
An amateur maker. He used a rather long and narrow model, and the work is
reasonably good but his varnish is very dark. It looks as though the wood was
stained before the varnish was applied. Stamped NOBLE under the button. The
tone is loud and shrill.

NOCK W.   *Oldbury*
He worked c. 1830. Reasonable work using plainish woods, ink lines for
purfling, gold brown varnish nicely applied.

NOON Thomas M.   *Cardiff*
He worked c. 1990 and made several good instruments.

NORBORN John   *London*
He worked c. 1720 not very great work with dark brown varnish.

NORMAN Barak 1688 - 1740   *London*
He was apprenticed to Urquhart and his early instruments resemble those of his
teacher. Later he adopted a small Maggini model but in fact he made relatively
few violins. His violas are excellent and of a good large size which makes them
sought after to-day. His 'cellos are generally small in size, around 718mm is
common, and they are decorated with purfling embellishments with a floral
design top and bottom and, often, a geometric design in the centre. The width
between the top circles of the soundholes is wider than usual, the soundholes
are set near to the edge and on the slant and the purfling rather broad.

NORMAN W.   *London*
A beautifully written repairers label read "Repaired by/W. Norman/Violin
Maker/5 Union St.,/London 1889". His work is not known to me.

NORRIS John 1739 - 1818   *London & Bath*
He was a pupil of Thos. Smith but made few instruments being more
concerned with commerce in partnership with R. Barnes. Instruments bearing
their label or branded NORRIS & BARNES were made by others and the quality
of the work varies according to the workman who produced it.

NORRIS William b1727 - d1798   *Wood Norton*
He was Rector of Wood Norton and learned violin making while in Nurnburg.
He made about two dozen instruments on his coming to Wood Norton, these
are very like violins of the Kloz school and are well made. Labelled and "N"
branded on the button.

NUNN Ernest S.   *Dagenham*
An amateur maker who produced about 60 instruments of good workmanship
and which he used to advertise in the 'Strad' in the years 1930 - 1960.

ODAM Charles   *Dartmouth*
He worked circa 1910 - 1920 using the Stradivarius model very effectively. The
materials and workmanship are good and neatly finished. His output was small.
Label in excellent calligraphy "Charles Odam No. 7/Dartmouth 1918".

OLDFIELD William   *Westmorland*
Worked c. 1900 using a Stradivarius model, handsome woods and an orange
brown varnish; refined workmanship.

OLD William   *Falmouth*
He worked around the period 1875 to 1905 at Chapel Place, Falmouth. The
model of his violins is large, workmanship quite good but not exceptionally so.
Biggish scroll scooped in quickly at the end of pegbox. Dark varnish, tone loud
and coarse.

OLDHAM Thomas c. 1820   *Tewkesbury*

OLIVER James c. 1820   *Reading*

O'MAHONEY James   *Mitchetstown, Cork*
He was an amateur maker, whose productivity was about 60 violins.

OMOND James 1833 - 1907   *Stromness*
He made about 300 violins, violas and 'cellos of good workmanship but the
tone is muffled owing to the plates being left too thick. He frequently varnished
them a 'brick' shade of red and this varnish has crackled; other colours of his
varnish seem to have avoided this fault.

OPIE A.J.   *Portsmouth*
An amateur who made a number of good violins. M/S label "4/Made by A.J.
Opie/Portsmouth 1918". Some of his instruments are a shade on the small side.

ORCHARD Joseph c. 1845   *Worchester*

ORR William c. 1910   *Broxburn*

ORTON Philip c. 1850   *Hereford*

OSBORNE Henry c. 1860   *Sherborne*

OSBORNE Samuel   *Leamington Spa*
A cabinet maker who made a few violins, violas, 'cellos and Basses.

OSMOND William   *Evesham*
c.1820 His work is very variable in quality.

OTTLEY Jacob   *Bristol*
Worked c. 1800 and his work is said to be good.

OUTRAM Frederick   *Leeds*
Quite well made violins. His name is written inside the back. His instruments
reputedly sound well. He worked c.1820.

OWEN Ivy Rimmer b.1883   *Leeds*
Daughter and pupil of J.W. Owen and her work is very much like his.

OWEN John William 1852 - 1933   *Leeds*
Initially self taught he later had some tuition in France. His work is excellent,
one of the best makers of his period. He made 149 violins, 12 violas and 53
'cellos. His workmanship is first class on a model which combines points
from Stradivarius and Guarnerius although generally a little longer in body
length. He was a first class repairer. Tonally his results were good. English
instruments so good as these are undervalued by comparison with quite
indifferent continental - especially Italian - productions of the same period.

OWERS J.A. c.1890   *Cambridge*
Poor work.

OXLEY Joseph   *Cambridge*
He worked c. 1800. His violins have a long body and high arching with shallow
ribs and brown varnish. The tone is soft and sweet. Branded J. Oxley or Oxley
under the button.

PADDOW W.R. b.1905   *Bingley*
He was an amateur maker who made about 40 instruments of average
workmanship. Label W.R. Paddow/No. 6 Bingley 1944".

PAGE Arthur Lewis b.1879   *Uxbridge*
He was an amateur maker. His violins on the Stradivarius model are made from
good materials and with very fair workmanship.

PAGE A.W. c.1900   *Darlington*

PAMPHILON Edward   *London*
He worked on London Bridge c.1680. His violins are made with very carefully
finished workmanship on a small highly arched model, sometimes double
purfled and varnished with a brilliant yellow varnish. The violas he made are
small.

PANORMO Edward Ferdinand 1811-1891 *London*
The son of Joseph and trained with Louis. He opened his own shop in Frith St. in 1840 but moved from one place to another never staying in one place for long. He made some violins but they are not highly regarded. It is as a guitar maker that he is best known.

PANORMO George I 1777-1852 *London*
Brother of Joseph. He specialised in guitars but also made violins, violas and 'cellos. Not all of the violins are good, in fact the quality is very variable but the best are excellent in every way. They are based on a Stadivarius model but not exactly so. For the best good materials are used and these are varnished a golden yellow having a trace of red in the shade. They are hardly ever labelled. The 'cellos also vary in quality but less so than with the violins, they are on a small pattern (735mm) and fairly highly arched: when labelled it is something simple like "PANORMO fecit London' which is not much help. He also made bows which are liked, often not stamped but when they are there is sometimes confusion since the stamp is L. PANORMO; they may be recognised by the very wide chamfer on the front of the head.

PANORMO George Lewis II 1815-1877 *London*
He made mainly guitars but also built a few good violins. Label "G. PANORMO-Fils/Fecit Londini, 1856". He worked first at 87 John St. and moved to 30 Whitfield St. in 1868.

PANORMO Joseph 1768-1834 *London*
Eldest son of Vincenzo. Worked with his father and also on his own in King Street. He made many guitars but also violins of vary variable workmanship, like George's the best are very good. His violins are unlabelled. Many instruments made for dealers such as Davis and Astor.

PANORMO Louis 1784-1862 *London*
Son of Vincenzo. Specialised in guitars but also made some very good violin bows stamped L. PANORMO. The sticks are mostly octagonal and the top and bottom facets of the stick are continued on to the front and back of the head. The sticks are, like those of Dodd, on the short side but the bows although rather rough play well.

PANORMO Vincenzo Trusiano 1734-1813 *Principally London*
In his early days he worked in several places commencing in Cremona with a descendant of Carlo Bergonzi. He finally settled in London in 1791 being employed by John Betts. His violins are copies of Stradivarius and the best are very good indeed. The workmanship if examined critically is not always good in some details, for instance the soundholes are often indifferently cut with small nicks and the fluting of the lower wings poorly done, but these little discrepancies do not detract from the work as a whole. The varnish of the early instruments is nothing much as it is thin with little colour and sometimes of a slightly greenish tinge derived, no doubt, from the ground colour. Later varnish is much more coloured, generally dark red/brown and tends to chip. The violas are mainly 380mm or just a shade longer and too small for true viola tone, but he made some, possibly for Betts, which are 407mm in body length and these are good. 'Cellos are very fine of handsome woods and with rather overlapping edges: the tone of his 'cellos is good. He also made some double basses which

are highly regarded. He used various labels and frequently no label at all which is understandable in making cheap instruments of inferior wood, and there are plenty of these ascribed to him, but less understandable when the product is good. Some are branded with his name, and 'cellos often have 'VP' branded by the tailgut

PARKER Daniel b.1680   *London*
He worked from about 1705-1760. It is not known from whom he learned to make violins. Early instruments follow the prevalent Amati pattern but he later abandoned this and used the Long Strad model as his guide, they are not exact copies. He made many instruments for the trade ranging from common to good according to the price received. His best instruments are 362mm body length with full and rounded edges, handsome woods, and all details of workmanship well done. The varnish is clear and satisfactory although some are varnished with a thick reddish shade (or red brown) not too well applied and often streaky.

PARKER George Arthur b.1874   *Wood Green*
Worked around 1895-1925. Stradivarius model effectively handled.

PARKINSON James   *Llandudno*
An amateur maker who made excellent instruments based on the Strad model. He also made violas and some 'cellos. Label M/S "James Parkinson/ No. 57 'Isis' A.S. model/1925".

PARSLOW T. c.1935   *New Cross*
Probably an amateur maker, fair work.

PATERSON James   *Llandudno*
Worked c.1925, quite reasonable work

PATERSON James 1834 - 1898   *Edinburgh*
A joiner who towards the last decade of his life became a professional maker having made violins as a hobby. His work is good on classical lines and generally varnished red/brown. Printed label "James Paterson/Edinburgh 1893 (J.P) ".

PAYNE Ralph   *South Shields*
Worked c.1900-1925 on a large Stradivarius style model.

PAYTON F. & W.C.   *Islington*
They owned a music shop in Camden Passage until about 1974. F. Payton made a few violins of average merit.

PEARCE George 1820-1856   *London*
He worked for Forster until his early death but no instruments bearing his name are known to the author.

PEARCE James   *London*
He worked in Saffron Hill about 1790; his instruments are not good.

PEARCE Thomas   *London*
He worked with his brother James and turned out much the same sort of work.

PEARCE Sleightholme b.1865   *Lincoln*
An amateur maker who used the Strad model, average work.

PEARCE William   *London*
He worked for Forster (unrelated to George Pearce) and his work is quite good.

PEARCE William R.   *London*
He worked c.1885. While his violins look all right they do not sound at all good.

PENNY Francis c.1927   *London*

PERHAM Walter James b.1883   *New Haw*
He was a pupil of Channon and a cabinet maker who produced about 30 violins based on Stradivarius or Guarnerius patterns.

PERRY James   *Kilkenny*
Cousin of Thomas and worked c. 1790. His work is rather rough but not clumsy in any way, generally unpurfled and varnished dark brown. He made violins, violas (small in size) and 'cellos. The latter roughly made, 'ink line' purfling and very wide between the top circles of the soundholes. Label "Made by James Perry/Kilkenny No. 509 1791" and stamped "PERRY/KILKENNY' below the button.

PERRY Joseph   *Dublin*
Cousin of Thomas who worked about 1800; he made some very good instruments and was a prolific maker it is said.

PERRY Thomas 1744-1818   *Dublin*
He carried on the business started by his father from whom he received his training. First instrument dated 1760. The number of instruments he made is a matter for speculation, the highest number on a label which the author has seen recorded is 4233 dated 1815. To produce this number required assistance and many instruments may have been made in part or whole by others, notably one Wilkinson whose name appears on tickets as Perry & Wilkinson. Work labelled Perry is very variable in quality and this may explain the variability. The best work is very good indeed. His violins are easily recognised by an unfailing characteristic in the soundholes viz. a small top circle, narrow stem at the top opening up all the way to the bottom turn - the soundholes are often set too high up the belly (commonly 188mm) and this characteristic is followed by Tobin his pupil (q.v.). Many of his violins are unlabelled, others labelled "Thos. Perry and Wm. Wilkinson" or "Perry" alone. Some printed, some manuscript as in "Tho.Perry/Christchurch Yard/Dublin 1767 No. 315". Many are branded PERRY/DUBLIN below the button but this brand is applied indiscriminately to continental violins as well. He made some violas and a few 'cellos, the latter very rare. The business continued until 1839 with Wilkinson in charge but there is a distinct falling off in quality after 1818 so it may be assumed that Thos Perry, if not making all of the instruments, nevertheless had a fairly strict supervisory position over what was turned out with their label.

PERRY W.J. *London*

Mainly a repairer but he made a few violins c. 1980.

PETHERICK Horace William b.1839 d.1919 *Croydon*

He made a few violins on an original model but is best known for some books he wrote which were published by the 'Strad' library. That on the "Repair and Restoration of Violins" contains much useful advice.

PETRIE James *Dundee*

He worked c. 1920 but his work is not very good.

PHILIP William *Bathgate (Scotland)*

He worked c. 1890 as an amateur maker who made some very nice instruments.

PHILIPS David b.1845 *Haverfordwest*

c. 1900. His instruments have a high arching and are of average workmanship. He was instructed by J.H. Whiteside.

PHILLIPS John b.1863 *Ynysybwl*

A cabinet maker who made some good violins in the period 1898 to 1925.

PHILIPSON Edward b.1859 *Aspatria*

An amateur maker who was self taught and made about 30 violins of very reasonable workmanship based on the Stradivarius model. They have one piece backs and open grained fronts generally, the model is rather on the full side both in length (365mm) and width. The varnish is an oil one, golden yellow and reddish orange. Label "E. PHILLIPSON/No. 13. 1907". He also made some bows in the Tubbs style.

PICKARD Handel *Leeds*

Worked c.1860. He was an amateur maker who achieved quite a reputation in his day for making and repairing. His violins rather highly arched and varnished deep golden brown. Label "Handel Pickard/School Close/Leeds 1862". Sometimes stamped H.PICKARD/LEEDS under the button.

PIERCE Frank Allen John b.1908 *Eastbourne*

A pupil of F.G. Richards. Originally a joiner who turned to violin making: he did not make many instruments but these are good. Printed label "Made by/Frank Allen John Pierce/of/Eastbourne/England 1952".

PIERCE Lyman A. 1858-1932

A self taught amateur who made over 30 good instruments, taught and played the violin and carried out repairs.

PIKE William d. circa 1960 *Exeter*

An amateur maker who Italianised his name on his labels to "Guliemus Pike, Exonensis". Schoolmaster and organist. He was taught by Geo. Wulme-Hudson and made about 30 violins of good workmanship.

PITT Darker b.1891 *Southport*

Amateur, self taught. Fair work.

PLAIN Walter 1804-1879 *Glasgow*
He was a cabinet maker who adopted violin making as a whole time occupation with success. He worked at 21 Brunswick Place, Glasgow and later (1875) moved to a small shop in Wilson Street. The model is on Stradivarius lines but not exactly so, edges nicely rounded but the arching crossways is sometimes rather 'pinched', inside of the ribs left quite rough, golden/brown hard varnish. Various labels "Walter Plain/Violin Maker/21 Brunswick Street/Glasgow 1871" or "WALTER PLAIN/Violin and Violoncello Maker/21 Brunswick Place, Glasgow 1852". He made several very nice 'cellos.

PLATT A.W. b.1873 *Bradford*
He was an amateur maker who made a few quite good instruments generally a deep golden brown in colour.

POLLARD Edwin *Blackpool*
He made his first violin in 1863 and was still working in 1925. His violins are mostly modelled after Stradivarius and the workmanship is good; his 'cellos are also on Stradivarian lines. Mostly his instruments are varnished shades of golden brown. He also made a few bows.

PORTER T. *Bishopwearmouth*
It is not known whether he made instruments. A label in a 'cello probably early 19th century read "T.PORTER/10 Watworth Street, Bishopwearmouth/ Dealer in Musical Instruments also repairer and tuner". Most probably he had instruments made for him.

POULTON R. *Hull*
Little is known of this maker but an example dated 1818 was on a Stradivarius pattern slightly modified and well made. Label "R. POULTON/Musical Instrument Maker/Chapel Lane, Hull, 1818".

POWELL G. *Bridlington*
He worked c. 1935. Known only by a well made 'cello using very handsome woods for the back, ribs and head and covered with a deep red and rather soft varnish somewhat patchily applied. The tone was loud but lacked sweetness. M/S label in capitals.

POWELL John *London*
He worked c.1790 in Clements Lane. His work is unknown to the author but it is said to be good using a dark red varnish. Probably related to Thomas.

POWELL Thomas *London*
He worked for Forster then opened a shop in Clements Lane with his brother Royal. He was employed from here by Forster as an outworker. His violins are nicely made, red brown in colour and have a small but pleasant tone. Violas follow the normal pattern of the day and are only about 380m body length.

POWELL Thomas Royal b.1791 *London*
He worked at 7 Borl Alley. Son of Thomas.

PRESTON James *London*
Whether or not he actually made the instruments bearing his name is not certain; there are many of them and the style and workmanship is variable although never of a high standard. The tables are often broad grained deal or red pine and the backs are seldom figured, purfling nearly always omitted and ink lines substituted. Label "J. Preston/Violin and Bass Maker/ Strand, London,1789".

PRESTON James c.1900 *Gomersal, Leeds*

PRETTS A. *London*
Pupil and assistant of S.A. Forster and his work is excellent.

PRICE Albert Henry *London*
He was principally a repairer, but, as a pupil of James Tubbs, he also made bows.

PRICE Reginald Gordon d. circa 1960 *New Malden*
His instruments are made from good materials with great care but the pale varnish that he employed does not do the fine workmanship justice.

PRIESTLY T.W. c.1970 *Clayton*

PRIESTNALL John 1819-1899 *Rochdale*
He was a cabinet maker who made about 350 instruments in all. The workmanship is reasonably good and the materials often handsome but it is spoiled by his varnish, a nondescript golden yellow which still seems soft and dull. His name etc. within an ornate border is stamped deeply on the back twice and the number of the instrument on the button - a quite tasteless method.

PRIOR William *Newcastle*
Finely finished work with his own label but it is conjectured that these violins were made by Edward Lewis, London.

PRINCE E.R. *Edenbridge*
No. 126 was dated 1941 but the workmanship was not good.

PRINCE W.B. b.1856 d.1926 *Tooting, London*
Very nicely made violins and 'cellos. He was a pupil of Glenister and, like his master, some essential dimensions of his 'cellos are incorrect. The workmanship using the Strad model is good in every way but frequently the dark red varnish on some of the instruments is now very badly crackled. He worked first at 17 Fircroft Road, later transferring to 227 Francescan Road, Upper Tooting. Label "W.B. Prince/Luthier/227 Francescan Road, Upper Tooting, S.W./No. 60 1924"

PROUT Ernest H. *Hounslow*
c. 1920. Mainly repairs but also made a few violins No. 3 being dated 1920.

PULLAR E.F. b.1872 *Plumstead*
Working period about 1898-1925 at 31 Vanbury Road, S.E. Basically Guarnerius style with sharply upturned edges and long corners nicely done. Varnish deep red/brown on a golden ground. Good work all round.

PURDAY T.E. *London*
He was in partnership first with Button and later with B.S. Fendt around 1800-1850. He made some instruments himself but these are of little merit. When he collaborated with Fendt the instruments labelled jointly were excellent. To what extent he, Purday, had a hand in their making is not known but considering Purday's earlier work it is likely that Fendt was mainly responsible. The later 'cellos are particularly good.

PYCROFT Ernest c.1870 *Manchester*
His work is reputedly good.

PYE J.A. c. 1925 *Liverpool*

PYNE George 1852-1921 *London*
A violinist who became a well known maker. Worked for many years for Edward Withers from his home in West Ham supplying them with new, frequently reproduction, instruments. Made over 500 violins but the author has never seen a viola: he made one 'cello. His work is generally good, the materials often plainish (but his prices were low), and the varnish not exactly exciting being a dullish yellow brown shade. His instruments are labelled and frequently branded G.PYNE, LONDON inside the back.

RADCLIFFE A.H. *Liverpool*
Amateur maker c. 1925 whose work is not good.

RAE John *London*
A cabinet maker who made violins first as a hobby and later full time from 1869 to about 1927. He made about 135 violins also a few violas and 'cellos. His work is well carried out and carefully finished but the tone is far too woody owing to excessive thickness in the construction: this can, of course, be rectified by a competent repairer: it is a great pity since otherwise his work is so good.

RAEBURN Alexander 1841-1907 *Leven*
Good workmanship on Stradivarius and Guarnerius models.

RAEBURN George R. 1846-1918 *West Calder & Leven*
A skilled and careful worker on Stradivarius and Guarnerius models, oil varnish by Whitelaw or Harris. Label "George R. Raeburn fecit/West Calder A.D.1899".

RAEBURN James 1810-1878 *Braco (Perthshire)*
A gardener by trade. Made many excellent instruments including some 'cellos.

RAEBURN John 1833-1910 *Largoward*
Eldest brother of Alexander & George. He commenced violin making as a hobby in 1856 and was self taught. He made about 100 violins and these are somewhat heavily but very neatly made. He worked certainly up to 1906.

RAISTRICK John W. *Bradford*
An amateur maker who worked c. 1910 and whose work is good.

RAITT J. c.1820 *Carphin, Fife*

RAMSEY William b.1869   *Biggar*
He made few instruments but these are well made, finely finished and covered with a good oil varnish of dark yellow shade. The materials used are of good quality. Label "W. Ramsey/Biggar/1897".

RATCLIFFE Harry Wynn   *Lockwood, Huddersfield*
He worked c. 1930-1960 and was a semi-professional maker. His work is well made but the edges are rather over strongly raised. The varnish he used is an oil one and inclined to softness, golden colours seem to be preferred. He published a short lived magazine for violin makers. Label "Harry Winn Ratcliffe/Lockwood 1945".

RAWLINS Henry   *London*
He worked c. 1780 and made violins, violas and 'cellos which are satisfactory but not outstanding in any way. The varnish is good, fairly thick in texture and of a rich colour.

RAYMAN Jacob   *London*
He worked c. 1620-1650 and came from the Tyrol. He is regarded as the founder of the English school. The violins are small in size and highly arched, short straight soundholes, small scroll, nice edges and corners and a good golden varnish. His 'cellos are highly regarded although still highly built.

RAYMENT A.F. b.1861   *London*
An amateur maker who worked between about 1900 and 1930; his work is good.

RAYMOND Robert John   *Bulmer*
An amateur maker whose work is average. c.1960.

READSHAW Jacob   *Middleton in Teesdale*
He worked c.1910. His work, both violins and violas, is very nicely made and covered with an excellent transparent golden varnish.

READ Arthur   *London*
Working c. 1930. His work is good. Label "Arthur Read/London/March 1930".

READ John R.W.   *London*
A pupil of Wulme-Hudson and, like him, made many reproduction violins often labelled with authentic Italian names. The work (violins, violas and 'cellos) is of fine quality. He worked at Walthamstow around the period 1930-1948. The varnish work let him down sometimes (as also Wulme-Hudson), since it is occasionally now badly crazed. Often his instruments are branded J. READ inside on the lower block and the name written on the face of the neck under the fingerboard.

REDDEN J. b.1860   *Duns (Berwick)*
Cabinet maker who made a few well made violins.

REDFERN William   *London*
Worked c.1830 on the Stradivarius model and that quite effectively. His materials are not the best, brownish varnish rather dull and tonally very average.

REED B. *Durham*
First quarter 20th century.

REED George c.1936 *London*
Probably an amateur, quite good work.

REED Joseph b.1882 *Barrow in Furness*
Worked at 17 Davy Street and made violins on the Stradivarius and Guarnerius models.

REEDY Joseph W. b.1822 *Barrow-in-Furness*
A little known maker.

REEGAN —. *Limerick*
Amateur maker c.1800 and fairly proficient.

RETFORD W.C. b.1875
Apprenticed to and worked for Hill's all of his life, retiring in 1956. In retirement he continued to make bows stamped with his name. His work is first class.

RETFORD W.R.
Son of W.C. Apprenticed to and worked for Hill's.

RHYS James b.1909 *Bridgend*
Pupil of Schlieps.

RICHARDS Edwin 1859-1894 *London*
His work is reputedly good.

RICHARDS Frederick George 1876-1966 *Eastbourne, Tunbridge Wells & Torrington*
He was an architectural woodcarver who made about 40 violins and 12 violas of good average workmanship. He worked at Torrington in a shed in the local churchyard, he then living in the almshouses opposite. In the selection of woods his instruments are attractive and they are nicely varnished. Towards the end of his life he made some excellent bridges which he sold to other makers under the name "Fiddlecraft".

RICHARDS Philip *London*
Worked in Wardour St., and later Noel Street. His violins and violas are very well made.

RICHARDSON Arthur 1882 - 1958 *Crediton*
He is regarded as one of the best modern English violin makers. Self taught he made a few violins while living in Leeds. Coming to live in Crediton to work for a firm of ecclesiastical woodcarvers he continued making and, having won the Cobbet prize for the best toned modern British violin, decided in 1919 to become a professional maker. He made 291 violins, 177 Tertis/Richardson violas, 30 violas on more conventional models and 32 'cellos. The 177 violas resulted from a collaboration commenced in 1937 with Lionel Tertis which resulted in the design of the Richardson/Tertis viola - an instrument of large

body and deep ribs: this enjoyed immense popularity for three decades but it is now out of fashion since the large size has presented problems to players using them. His instruments are always well made and he was a perfectionist in every detail. In the matter of varnishing he was not always successful since some coatings have begun to craze, he used both Milington's varnish and one which he prepared himself. Frequently the tone of his violins is very clear and brilliant but of no great quality.

RICHMOND Malcolm F.   *Falkirk*
Worked c. 1925. Quite nice work.

RIDGE Eric V.   *Gloucester*
Working c. 1945. M/S label.

RILEY Henry c.1920   *Birmingham*
His work is said to be good.

RIMBAULT H.E.   *Cardiff*
Amateur in 1920.

RIPPENGALL C.W.   *Leicester*
A dentist and amateur violin maker who worked from about 1935 to 1955 and produced very reasonable work including several Tertis model violas.

RIPPON Alfred Ferdinand   *Reading*
He worked c. 1870 on a Stradivarius model with deep ribs. Golden yellow/brown varnish. Bows stamped A.E. RIPPON are sometimes seen: these are probably of German manufacture.

RIPPON Alan   *Stamford*
Son of John Rippon. Worked c. 1890 and branded A. RIPPON below the button.

RIPPON John   *Peterborough*
Worked c. 1840. Made several quite good violins some of which have female heads (one labelled Alan Rippon treated thus).

RITCHIE Alexander b.1873   *Laurencekirk*
Made about 20 violins of average workmanship.

RITCHIE Alexander b.1888   *Battersea*
Amateur who worked from about 1925 to 1950. His workmanship was good using best materials, the plates left just a shade too thick for best tonal emission.

RITCHIE Archibald b.1833 d.1902   *Dundee*
Made about 200 violins principally on the lines of Guarnerius but the dimensions slightly larger, the edges thick and raised and a generally slightly heavy appearance about the whole. Usually nicely figured back wood and the instruments covered with an oil varnish inclined to be chippy. Labelled and stamped A. RITCHIE inside the back and/or below the button.

RITCHIE John   *Aberdeen & Dundee*
Made violins and violas c. 1880.

RITCHIE William J.   *Bonnybridge*
He worked c. 1930. His violins are in the style of Guarnerius but a shade larger, the workmanship excellent and covered with an oil varnish favouring a red/brown shade.

RITCHIE William   *Alva*
Worked c. 1870. His violins are on a large Stradivarius model, often over 362mm body length; they are fairly well made from figured woods. Label "Wm.Ritchie/Maker/1867/Alva".

ROBERTS Alexander c.1910   *Laurencekirk*
Amateur worker and very good work.

ROBERTS A.J. b.1873   *London*
Made about 20 violins which are very well made. He started the British Violin Makers Guild in West End Lane in 1910 and this venture brought to the front several hitherto unknown makers.

ROBERTS John c. 1690   *Shrewsbury*
Stainer pattern.

ROBERTS Lewis 1868-1910   *Morriston, Swansea*
He made violins on a large Stradivarius model with fair workmanship c.1900. (No. 40 dated 1910).

ROBERTS John c.1700   *Shrewsbury*

ROBERTS Ronald b1912   *Exeter*
Woodwork tutor and talented violin maker who made violins and violas of excellent workmanship. He also made other instruments such as lutes, rebecs and one viol.

ROBERTS R.C.   *Bolton*
Worked c. 1880, his work is of little consequence.

ROBERTSON John   *Blairgowrie*
Worked c. 1850-1870, his work is not good.

ROBERTSON John   *Rannock*
Worked c. 1935. His violins are based on the model of Joseph Guarnerius and are carefully made. No. 11 dated 1937.

ROBERTSON John   *Edinburgh*
Probably an amateur maker but his instruments are excellent. Worked c. 1890.

ROBINS F. d.1890   *Pilton, Barnstaple*
Amateur whose productivity was large but not very impressive.

ROBINSON Alfred George b.1879 *Willingdon*
Made few instruments both violins and violas (the latter 422mm body) and these are of average amateur workmanship.

ROBINSON Stanley d.1968 *Abbey Wood*
Son of William. Trained as a woodcarver and, after the War was employed on reproduction woodcarving in the style of Grinlin Gibbons in London churches which had been bombed. Made a few instruments in Abbey Wood both in collaboration with his father and personaly labelled. Moved to Devizes about 1952 but made no instruments there.

ROBINSON William 1880-1964 *Plumstead*
Self taught maker who achieved considerable success and was a prolific maker. His first instrument is dated 1908 whilst working at Woolwich Arsenal. He decided to become a professional maker and on his death had made 420 violins, 40 violas and 15 'cellos. Winner of the Cobbett prize for the best toned modern British made violin in 1923 after which his instruments were in demand both at home and abroad; several well known soloists used them. His work shows touches of the lack of a formal trade apprenticeship but is not lacking in finish. The violins are never oversize and on a model which combines points from Italian masters, a personal feature is that he liked to surround the button with an ebony crown a bit larger than is usual. His violas are mostly 400mm although he made a few over 405mm. The 'cellos are well made but far too heavy and full of wood to sound well. He always used an oil varnish and unlike many makers contemporary with him, never appears to have had problems of crazing with it. He never varnished an instrument to simulate wear. His instruments are labelled (printed) "William Robinson/Plumstead,London/A.D. 1922/No. 69. W.R. (Added in ink)".

ROBSON A *London*
Worked c. 1870, his work is reputedly good.

ROGERS George *Belfast*
Worked c. 1910 and his work is excellent. No. 9 dated 1910.

ROGERS George *Conlig Co. Down*
1925. Excellent work on the Stradivarius model.

ROLFE Eric b1912 *Exmouth*
Amateur maker, physicist and artist. Made a few violins and two violas circa 1980.

ROOK Joseph 1777 - 1852 *Carlisle*
An amateur working c. 1810 - 1850 who made about 40 violins, 12 violas and 5 'cellos. He wrote his name inside the belly and very often stamped them J. ROOK/CARLISLE under the button. The work is quite neat and the varnish a yellow brown or red brown in colour.

ROPE Alfred James 1862 *Woolwich*
A self taught maker who completed over 200 instruments, violins, violas and 'cellos during the period about 1890 - 1930. These are rather heavily built and of average workmanship frequently not improved in appearance by the light coloured varnish.

ROSS Donald 1817 - 1901   *Edinburgh*
An amateur who made about 50 violins of fair workmanship generally on the Maggini model. They are unlabelled and not marked with any identification.

ROST Franz Georg 1869 - 1960   *London*
He lived in London from 1903 - 1922 and from 1932 to his death. His work is very good. He used various labels "Franz Georg Rost/London 1937" "Franz Georg Rost/13 Amery Row, Brook St.,/London W. 1913" etc. and sometimes branded them F.G. ROST LONDON on the inner back.

ROUSE J. c. 1810   *Oakham*

ROWE John   *Taunton*
An amateur working c. 1870 - 1885. He made about a dozen violins of excellent workmanship covered with a soft slightly crackled varnish.

ROWE Thomas A. b1909   *Cowes*
An amateur maker who followed the Guarnerius pattern. No. 9 dated 1909.

ROWLEY Arthur John b1880   *Coventry & Northampton*
A violin teacher and professional maker and repairer who made over 100 instruments of good workmanship, nicely finished and attractively varnished. No. 97 dated 1932. He also made a few bows branded A.J. ROWLEY.

RUDDIMAN Joseph 1733 - 1810   *Aberdeen*
Early instruments from 1760 are highly arched, thinly wooded, quite well made and have a small sweet tone. Later ones are on Stradivarius lines but larger, ribs deep, plates thin, often 'ink line' purfling and a forbiddingly dark varnish. 'cellos are rather better in quality, but on the whole his work is not of a high standard. He was a prolific maker.

RUDDOCK –.   *Manchester*
Said to be a pupil of Craske, but I have not seen any of his work.

RUNNACLES H.E.   *Stowmarket*
He worked as an amateur maker and repairer during the period 1960 - 1980.

RUSHWORTH & DREAPER   *Liverpool*
See under 'ARDETON'.

RUSSELL William   *Leeds*
Worked c. 1830 but not very well.

RUSSEL William   *Banff*
A carpenter who made a few violins as an amateur.

SABY Henry Humphrey   *Nottingham*
A pupil of W. Calow for five years then made and repaired violins in Nottingham until 1890 when he left for Cape Town where he prospered as a maker, dealer and repairer.

SAINT-GEORGE George b1841   *London*
Made a few violins and viola da gambas.

SAMPLE Thomas E. b1880   *Ashington*
A joiner who produced several quite good violins period 1910 - 1925.

SARLE T. c. 1915   *London*

SAUNDERS Stephen 1840   *Twickenham*
Amateur making of excellent quality.

SAVAGE George   *Leicester*

SAXON John   *Stockport*
19th Century.

SAXTON Thomas   *Nottingham*
His violins were made on a large model 362mm body length. Small figured
woods and broad grained fronts. Label "Tho. Saxton/Nottingham 17/0" also
stamped T. SAXTON below the button.

SCARBROW A.   *London*
Bowmaker who worked for Hill's.

SCARFE Roland b1869   *Bexhill on Sea*
Worked C. 1920.

SCHILLER Emil   *London*
He worked at Castle St., 38 Berners Street and 15 Soho Square between about
1898 and 1912. His workmanship is excellent. The varnish is sometimes
crackled; in some respects his work is reminiscent of Szepessy Bela. Label "Emil
Schiller/Violin, Tenor and 'cello Maker/38 Berners St., London, W./1898". He
returned to Germany about 1938.

SCHOLES Arthur L. b1870   *Rushden, Bedford and London*
His first instrument dates from 1888. His work is good on Stradivarius and
Guarnerius models and covered with a good oil varnish. He was certainly
working up to 1941. Label "Made by/Arthur L. Scholes/Bedford. England/No.
96 1941".

SCHOLES F.L.   *Greenford*
Probably an amateur maker, his label reads "F.L. Scholes/Violin Maker/
Greenford, Middx, England/No.6 1948".

SCOTT Joseph   *Haltcliff Nr. Heskett*
Worked as an amateur c. 1780 - 1810 and made over 70 instruments. Good
workmanship and materials on a model akin to Stradivarius. The soundholes set
on the slant have a very straight sided stem. Well carved head the throat being
very open and the peg box cheek deep under the volute. Varnish deep red and
golden brown. He instructed Joseph Rook who was a servant to him in 1795.
Label "J. Scott/Haltcliff near/at Heskett New Market/Fecit". Sometimes stamped
SCOTT below the button.

SCULTHORPE   *Hanningworth*
Working c. 1840.

SEXTON John   *London*
In a violin of fair workmanship on a fairly highly arched model 362mm long was found the label "John Sexton/Fecit on London Bridge/from Mr. Collingwood - 1728": also branded below the button.

SEYMOUR   *Warwick and Leamington Spa*
c. 1880 Poor work.

SHACKLETON Daniel   *Bedford*
Worked c. 1890 and made both violins and violas of creditable workmanship and finish. The violas are 400mm body length. Varnish golden brown.

SHARP James   *Leeds*
c. 1875 Probably an amateur, fair work.

SHAW John   *Manchester*
Double bass player. Lived in Hulme, Manchester where he made some excellent violins during the period 1900 - 1915. He also made some miniature violins of 80mm body length and 132mm overall length complete with bow and case to match.

SHAW Thomas b1864   *Cove*
Amateur who made on the Stradivarius pattern. Label "Tom Shaw/Cove, Dumbartonshire" M/S.

SHELMERDINE Anthony   *Liverpool*
Amateur c. 1925. His work is excellent on the Stradivarius model using handsome wood and a golden brown oil varnish.

SHEPHERD William N. 1932 - 1986   *London*
A fairly prolific primarily self taught maker of violins, violas and 'cellos, he made over 120 instruments, mainly violas, of good quality as well as being very active as a repairer.

SHEPHERD M.J.   *London*
Son of the above. Bowmaker with Hill's whom he left in 1975.

SHEPLEY George   *Bristol*
c. 1830. Average class of work.

SHERDON Daniel   *Gloucester*
c. 1850. Exaggeratedly high arching and poor work.

SIMPSON Frank T. b1887   *Dunmow*
He used the Stradivarius model also an original one with a flat arching using handsome woods and applying a splendid oil varnish.

SIMPSON George S.   *Crail*
Made about 40 violins on a large Guarnerius pattern 362mm body length. The general workmanship is very satifactory as is the, generally, dark orange/brown oil varnish. Label "George S. Simpson/70 Nethergate/Crail.

SIMPSON John & James *London*
Father and son who worked together between about 1780 - 1800. The work is variable in quality yet even in the poorest it is usually found that the backs and ribs are of handsome wood frequently one piece and of narrow figure. The instruments are not always purfled. Doubt has been cast as to whether John, the father, was a maker, certainly some instruments with the joint label were made for them by Richard Duke, and probably other makers also supplied them.

SIMPSON Robert . 1925 *Belfast*

SIMPSON Robert *Falkirk*
Made large bodied violins with only moderate workmanship. No label but inscribed the back "Robert Simpson/fecit Falkirk 1828".

SIMPSON Thomas b.1866 *Peterborough, Birmingham & Brixham*
His first instruments date from about 1898 in Peterborough. He moved to Birmingham in 1900 working at 55 Thornhill Road, Handsworth where he made many violins and violas which although not the acme of refinement are, nevertehless, very satifactory: esteemed as a repairer. Moved to Brixham in 1925. The violins are on varying models, while the violas are 412mm body length. No 'cellos are known to me. He also made a few good bows stamped SIMPSON BIRMINGHAM.

SINCLAIR William b.1836 *New Pitsligo*
An amateur who worked until at least 1902 making about 40 violins on the Guarnerius model. The early ones are rather crude but his work speedily improved. Label "William Sinclair/New Pitsligo/Aberdeenshire. N.B./1902".

SIRRELL S.H. *Stratford-on-Avon*
Worked c. 1935 probably an amateur. The work is quite good.

SKEFFINTON William Kirkland b.1845 *Glasgow*
Made a quantity of violins as an amateur maker. While the workmanship is reasonably good the models that he followed (or his conception of them) are not, as a result the tone of his instruments is not liked. The varnish he used is of a peculiar crimson colour.

SKINNER John Walter 1868 - 1954 *Sheffield & Dawlish*
A cabinet maker who became a professional violin maker and repairer working in Sheffield from 1918 to 1930 then moving to Dawlish. He made 18 violins, the first eight in Sheffield the remainder in Dawlish the last one being made in 1942. His work is reasonably well finished. He used an oil varnish the last few instruments being varnished with Millington's varnish. Label "John Walter Skinner/Violin Maker, Sheffield/No.6 AD 1924". (Printed).

SLADE Joseph b1859 *South Godstone*
Amateur maker. Worked at violin making from 1886 to about 1925. His production though not large is of good quality.

SMART George   *London*
Worked c. 1720 in the Oxford Road. His work is generally well enough made but not especially so, frequently plainly wooded and normal purfling replaced by ink lines. He used a good varnish of red/orange or orange/brown shade. Stamped G. SMART below the button.

SMART John   *London*
c. 1700 His name is given in other directories and there may be evidence for his existence as a maker but possibly there is confusion with the previous entry.

SMILLIE Alexander b1847   *Glasgow*
A self taught professional maker who succeeded in his chosen work. His model is like the Stradivarius pattern but not exactly so. The conception is heavier, edges quite thick and nicely rounded, the plates left thick yet well tapered, nearly always well figured backs and all of the details well carried out. The varnish is not always too good being very inclined to chip. Label "Alex: Smillie fecit/Crosshill, Glasgow, 1895/No. 78". He made also violas and 'cellos one of the latter having a back with at least 42mm rise, the front less arched but still greater than normal; why this oddity?

SMILLE Andrew Young 1878 - 1948   *Glasgow*
Son of the above. He made over 200 violins as well as violas and 'cellos. His instruments are fine specimens as regards to workmanship but the model is not always good since some violins have a very stiffly shaped centre bout accentuated by markedly hooked corners all rather ugly: fortunately such instruments are in the minority. His violas measure generally just under 405mm in body length. The varnish, an oil preparation and less chippy than his father's, at least on later instruments, is generally an orange brown or red brown. Label "A. Smillie & Son/171 St. Georges Road, Glasgow/No. 214 - 1911".

SMITH Alexander Howland b1859   *Edinburgh*
Made about 50 violins on conventional models and of very satisfactory workmanship.

SMITH Arthur Edward   *Malden, later Sydney*
Made a few violins up to 1909 when he emigrated to Australia.

SMITH —.   *Sheffield*
Known only by a 'cello dated 1789, 743mm body, Wamsley style, the back with small Sheraton style inlay, the pegbox with stringing, inlay under the fingerboard, nicely figured woods, well made, golden brown varnish. Labelled from Sycamore Street, Sheffield and stamped "SMITH/SHEFFIELD" under the button.

SMITH Bert   *Coniston*
His violins which achieved fame in his lifetime are modelled after Guarnerius and Stradivarius; the violas are 420mm body length. The workmanship is good and the tone excellent. Worked from about 1930 to 1965.

SMITH Dennis G. b1919   *Ashstead*
Violin maker, dealer and repairer c. 1960 who worked at 51 The Street, Ashstead.

SMITH Edwin c. 1910   *Wetherby*

SMITH Horatio   *Kidderminster*
c. 1910 (No. 12 dated 1911).

SMITH James   *Coaltown of Wemyss*
Worked c. 1940 as a maker and repairer.

SMITH James   *London*
Worked c. 1725 on the Amati model. His work is quite satifactory.

SMITH James   *Chapelhall*
His work is variable in quality but is known for producing a splendid tone.
Working period c .1920.

SMITH John   *Whitchurch*
Worked c. 1800. Fine work on the Amati model. He made violins, violas and
'cellos the latter rather small in proportions and varnished with a fine golden
varnish.

SMITH John 1850 - 1923   *Teddington*
His violins are in the style of Guarnerius, carefully made and well finished
frequently using a fine deep red varnish. Label "Made by/John Smith/
Teddington/London, W." Worked c. 1800 - 1915.

SMITH John 1859 - 1941   *Falkirk, later Winnipeg*
A cabinet maker who began making violins in 1878. He decided to become a
professional maker working first in Falkirk until 1904 when he moved to
Glasgow finally emigrating to Canada. His best violins are in the style of
Guarnerius but more heavily conceived; the work throughout is of fine quality.
He was trained by John Carr in Falkirk. He used Whitelaw's varnish for all of
his work in this country. Various labels. "John Smith/Maker/Falkirk 1896".
Some idea of his productivity can be gauged by No. 26 being dated 1897 and
No. 50 1899. He made violins, violas and 'cellos.

SMITH John E. b1867   *London*
Pupil and assistant of Glenister. His output is small, well enough made without
being the acme of refinement and nicely varnished in shades of red/brown. In
addition to a label his name etc. is on the bottom rib under the varnish.

SMITH John Hey c. 1900   *Burnley*

SMITH M.F.   *Glasgow*
c. 1900. Probably an amateur maker, very reasonable work.

SMITH Nathaniel c. 1830   *Bristol*

SMITH Pye c. 1850   *Hereford*

SMITH Robert c. 1910   *Coatbridge*

SMITH Robert *Plymouth*
Known only by a "cello made from plain woods, average workmanship. Name
inscribed on inner back "Robert Smith/Plymouth 1888".

SMITH Thomas *London*
Pupil and successor of Peter Wamsley and worked c. 1740 - 1790. His violins
are of flattish arching, often narrow flamed sycamore for the backs and
varnished a light golden brown. He is best known for his 'cellos although these
really are very ordinary. They are generally made from plainish wood for the
backs etc., ink lines substitute for purfling and the varnish is a dirty yellow
brown colour. Sometimes labelled, and others just branded T. SMITH on the
back.

SMITH Thomas b.1901 *Larkhill*
Made about a dozen violins and two 'cellos circa 1920.

SMITH W. *Glasgow*
Worked c. 1860 on the Stradivarius model. His workmanship is good and the
tone also. Printed Label "W. Smith/Glasgow 1856".

SMITH Walter Napier b.1912 *Eastcote*
An amateur maker who took up the hobby late in life and made a few violins
and one viola. His work is good, carefully finished and tonally very satisfactory.

SMITH William c. 1800 *Hedon*

SMITH William *Glasgow*
Stradivarius model, neat work, yellow brown varnish. Printed label "W.
Smith/Glasgow 1858".

SMITH William c. 1780 *London & Sheffield*

SMITH William Edward *Wetherby*
c. 1904. He first worked in Leeds later moving to Wetherby, his later work is
good.

SMITH W.E. *Bristol*
In addition to making some good violins he prepared an excellent varnish.

SMITH William F. c.1900 *Edinburgh*

SMITHSON William *Stockport*
Known only by a well made 'cello 733mm body length, nicely figured back and
ribs, red deal belly, good model and purfling, long slanting soundholes, very
fine deep red varnish, excellent tone. Unlabelled but signed 1/S back "William
Smithson/Manchester Hill, Nr. Stockport, Lancashire 1799".

SOMMERVILLE William *Bathgate*
Made a quantity of well made and nicely finished violins first quarter 20th
century (No, 52 made in 1913). Label "W. Sommerville/Udale Cottage, Bathgate
1913 No. 52".

SOMNY Joseph Maurice d1931   *Hanwell*
Pupil of Somny-Ouchard. Worked for Hill's from 1888 - 1910 when he established himself at Boston Rd. Hanwell, later in George St., London. His work is variable but the best is very good. Noted as a fine restorer.

SORREL Frank d1927   *Welsey and Gt. Bentley*
Amateur maker of poor quality instruments.

SOUTHGATE W. c. 1890   *Birmingham*

SOWERBY A.L.   *Manchester*
c. 1900 - 1930. Professional maker, and repairer, good work.

SOWERBY D. c. 1910   *Thwaite*

SPARKES Nathaniel   *Bristol*
He had an ornate 'trade card' printed describing himself as a maker and repairer but no instrument made by him has been seen by the author.

SPIRES Stewart b1809 b1870   *Ayr*
Produced a good number of violins during the period 1840 - 1869. His early work is not satisfactory being thin in the plates and feeble in tone: the later work is much better. Label "Stewart Spiers/Maker, Ayr,/1862".

SPRING John c. 1930   *London*

STALLYBRASS Rev. H.M.   *Astley Abbotts*
He worked circa 1900 and made several violins of average amateur finish on an approximation to the Guarnerius model. Good choice of wood. Exaggeratedly long soundholes. Oil varnished quite well.

STANLEY Robert A. b1860   *Manchester*
He worked at 87 City Road and was a pupil of James Barrow and James Cole. He worked c. 1885 to 1924 and made a large quantity of violins, violas, 'cellos and double basses with good workmanship using good materials and a fine oil varnish. His work is for some reason commercially undervalued. Label "Robert A. Stanley/Violin & Bow Maker/Manchester 1900".

STANTON F.G. b1900   *Wanstead*
An amateur maker self-taught who made a few nicely constructed violins.

STEDMAN R.   *Leyton*
c. 1850 Good workmanship.

STEELE James   *Wallington*
A self taught amateur maker, working period 1920 - 1940. Stradivarius model, handsome woods and exemplary workmanship. M/S label "James Steele./Londonensis fecit July 1921".

STENT E. c.1914   *London*

STEVENS Thomas c. 1790   *Bristol*

STIRRAT David *Edinburgh*
He worked from about 1810 to 1826. Stradivarius outline with the arching a shade fuller, carefully finished work using good , but not always very figured, woods. Thin varnish probably spirit, yellow brown shades generally. Made violins, violas and 'cellos.

STOCKDALE William *Acklington*
Amateur maker. His violins generally follow the Guarnerius model. Worked c. 1880.

STOLBERG John 1881 - 1960 *Croydon*
A professional 'cellist with the Carl Rosa Opera Company. He was a pupil of George Buckman of Dover and completed 57 violins and 10 'cellos. These are well made and nicely finished.

STONEMAN Henry 1856 - 1932 *Exeter*
He was apprenticed to joinery and came to Exeter in 1876 to work for Luscombe and Sons ecclæsiastical furnishers with whom he stayed for 24 years. During this time he repaired violins as a hobby. In 1900 he established himself as a full time repairer and maker in Union Terrace, St. Sidwell's and his repair ticket is in countless instruments throughout Devon. He made only 12 violins, these are rather heavy in style (thick corners, strong edges etc.) but are well enough made. No. 8 was bought by Albert Sammons who used it for his recording of the Elgar violin concerto. He also produced excellent carving gouges which were hand forged, these he sold to other makers.

STOTT George Theodore b.1870 *Liverpool*
Initially took up violin making as a hobby but later decided to work professionally. He made about 80 instruments - violins, violas and a few 'cellos. His violins are rather heavy with strong upturned edges and wide corners but well enough done and nicely finished. The varnish is an oil one of a golden yellow shade, sometimes red. His 'cellos are in much the same style, very heavy and having peculiar shaped and over long soundholes. He worked between 1900 and about 1945. His son had a violin business in Bournemouth but only undertook repairs.

STOREY Herbert H. b.1885 *East Dulwich*
A self taught amateur maker and friend of George Buckman. His violins on the Strad model are quite well made and varnished red/brown.

STRATTON James *Skipton*
Amateur maker c. 1925.

STREETS James *Sunderland*
Amateur circa 1900: his work is said to be good but I have not seen any of it.

STROUD Cyril Charles *Etwall and Peterborough*
c. 1975.

STURGE H. *Bristol*
Worked c. 1810 in Stephen Avenue, Clare St., Bristol and later in Huddersfield. He may have been only a repairer.

STYLES Harold Lester 1900 - 1983   *Bath*
He was a pattern maker who took up violin making in 1960 and designed for
his use a 1:1 pantograph router to help shape the plates. The edges of his
instruments are thick and with a deep groove up to them. He made about 70
instruments, both violins and violas.

SWANSTON Leo b1868 d1906   *Newcastle*
Cabinet maker who made a few violins as a hobby.

SYMINGTON George   *Kilmarnock*
Worked c. 1880.

SZEPESSY Bela 1856 - 1925   *London*
He was apprenticed to Nemessanyi and later worked for Zach in Vienna before
coming to London in 1881. His instruments are first class, generally on the
Guarnerius model but also following Stradivarius. Dimensionally they frequently
vary from the originals thus we find Guarnerius style instruments having a body
length of 365mm. The varnish (apart from a few deep red coatings which have
badly crazed) is very fine, deep orange brown, and deep red - always rich. He
seemed to favour medium to broad grained wood for the tables of his
instruments. He also made some large violas and a few 'cellos. Mostly his
productions are dated and numbered (No. 11 - 1885, No. 246 - 1922). Sometimes
bows are seen branded SZEPESSY BELA; probably these are French productions.

TARR Aubrey James b1904   *Exmouth*
An amateur maker who produced excellent work between about 1930 and
1965 following principally the Stradivarius model. He made his own varnish
which looks very good but is inclined to be soft and a bit chippy. Made about
40 violins, 10 violas and 2 'cellos.

TARR Shelley   *Manchester*
Son of William Tarr.

TARR Joseph G. b1835   *Manchester*
Son of William who moved to New York in 1900. He made a few instruments
in this country including double basses which have a violin outline with
sloping shoulders.

TARR Thomas   *Sheffield*
Worked c. 1865 - 1899. A double bass player, maker, repairer and dealer. His
work is quite good but not excellent, the varnish, generally variations on
golden brown, is nicely laid on and polished. Label "Thomas
Tarr/Maker/Sheffield 1879".

TARR William 1809 - 1892   *Manchester*
Double bass player and professional maker of violins, violas, 'cellos and double
basses (supposed to have made over 200 of the latter). The violins are on a
fairly large pattern and quite well made as are his violas and 'cellos. The varnish
is at it's best a golden brown but many have a rather lifeless brown varnish
applied to them. Various labels and sometimes stamped on the back (No. 24 -
1876 and No. 208 - 1884).

TAWSE George   *Glasgow*
Worked circa 1935 - 1955 for part of this time with Smillie. He made about 50 violins and violas but the work is very amateurish and heavy. Typewritten label "George Tawse/Maker/Glasgow circa 1950".

TAYLOR Joseph c. 1905   *London*

TAYLOR Robert   *Leicester*
He worked between about 1912 - 1946. His violins are very well made, frequently with one piece backs handsomely flamed, the edges strong but not excessively so, well cut soundholes. Good finish and all covered by a fine oil varnish generally shades of red/brown. His violas are just over 405mm body length. He made a few 'cellos as well as some bows. Label "Robert Taylor/Maker/5 Ann St., Leicester/Anno 1912". Sometimes branded R. TAYLOR/LEICESTER below the button.

TAYLOR Stephen Oliver   *Leicester*
An organ builder who made a few stringed instruments circa 1910.

TAYLOR Thomas Duxbury   *Bolton*
Cabinet maker who produced a few quite good violins c. 1880.

TAYLOR William   *London*
He assisted Panormo. His violins are variable, some quite highly arched and thin in the belly, others of flatter modelling. Varnish golden/brown. The style is Amati like and on the higher arched models the arching is typically pinched at the bridge position: soundholes straight set and rather open. Often not labelled but the name written in ink inside the belly. He also made violas and 'cellos.

TEALE John   *London*
c. 1830. His instruments are rather nice.

TEMPLE George b1904   *Morpeth & Broomhill*
Excellent instruments on standard classical models. He also made a few Tertis model violas. Label "George Temple/Maker/Broomhill Northumberland 1931". Sometimes the name TEMPLE BROOMHILL is branded on the middle bout linings.

TEMPLE William   *Broomhill*
An amateur maker who made a few instruments and a fair number of bows. Brother of the above.

TEMPLE William   *Wimbledon*
Amateur maker c. 1900, his work is barely average.

TENNANT James   *Lesmahagow*
Made violins, violas and some 'cellos c. 1850 but they are not very good.

THERESS Charles   *London*
Principal assistant to Ch. Maucotel 1845. Worked on his own account in King St. Soho 1848 - 1860. Some of his work is personally labelled but he also worked for other makers when his name may be found pencilled inside the belly.

THIRLBY C.S.
Amateur maker c. 1910.

Romsey

THOMAS R.J.
Worked c. 1950.

Darlington

THOMAS Watkin 1849 - 1908

Swansea

A prolific maker but his work is very variable in quality. Some of his violins are of normal proportions but others are very large, occasionally they have a dragon's head in place of a scroll. Workmanship reasonably good but some examples not purfled. The violas he made are of normal size, 412mm frequently.

TOMPSETT J.A.

Folkstone

He was taught by Alfred Chanot and made a few violins and violas during the period 1950 - 1970.

THOMPSON A.

Edinburgh

Worked c. 1924. Reasonable work. Sometimes his instruments have decorated purfling. Label "A. Thompson/Maker/Edinburgh 1924".

THOMPSON Charles and Samuel

London

Sons and successors to Robert. It is not known for certain to what extent instruments bearing their label were actually made by them. That some must have been is logical but the violins vary so much in style and quality that other makers must have supplied them to a large degree. The better instruments are probably the work of Jacob Ford, less good ones by John Barton while even less good ones probably from the hands of various journeymen makers of the time. The name of David Furber has been found in one C & S Thompson labelled violin. The violas are generally quite good and even better are some of the 'cellos for some of these were made by Edmund Aireton. Instruments bearing their name date from about 1770 - 1810.

THOMPSON Edward F.M. b1892

Deal, Worthing & Cornwall

Pupil of Alfred Dixon. Commenced making instruments about 1918. His violins, and there are few of them, are mainly on the Guarnerius model, correct for size but of very average workmanship.

THOMPSON James

Crookham

Rather rustic and heavy looking instruments although using prettily figured wood on a near to Stradivarius outline, ink lines instead of purfling, spirit varnished and branded JT below the button. Period c. 1830.

THOMPSON James c. 1930

Old Heaton

THOMPSON James

London

Violins of a large Stradivarius model 364mm body length and of average workmanship. Working c. 1860. In Murton Square, London.

THOMPSON John c. 1750

London

THOMPSON John

London

Worked at Old Holborn c. 1840. Good work.

THOMPSON Robert *London*
Highly arched violins, but not excessively so, and rather thin in the plates. Some much better violins bear his name, whether or not he made them is open to conjecture since the standard is so much better, the backs handsome, full arching yet graceful and a good golden brown varnish. The 'cellos fall into the latter category, they are very nice examples of old English work. Period 1740 - 1770.

THOMPSON Samuel & Peter *London*
Samuel first worked with Robert, his father; then with Charles, his brother; and finally with Peter his son. The work bearing their name is very much of the Thompson 'middle class' variety. Like many other London makers of the time they made for the trade.

THOMPSON William *Bishop Aukland*
Amateur who worked c. 1870.

THOMSON W.M. *Dysart, Kirkalby*
A cabinet maker who completed a few nicely made instruments during the period 1910 - 1925; these are on the Stradivarius model, figured backs etc. and broad grained fronts all covered with an orange/brown varnish.

THOMSON James *Berwick on Tweed*
Only completed a few instruments as an amateur but these are nicely made.

THOMSON George c. 1860 *Aberdeen*

THORBURN S.W. *Symington Mill*
c. 1910 Mediocre work.

THORLEY N. *Failsworth, Manchester*
He made a good number of violins, violas and 'cellos during the period 1810 - 1850. Label "Made by/N. Thorley/Failsworth 1814".

THORLEY Thomas *Failsworth, Manchester*
Son of the above, and as good a maker. Worked c. 1870 - 1885. He made violins, violas and 'cellos one of the latter having a finely figured whole back cut on the quarter. This unlabelled but Thos. Thorley/Failsworth 1877 signed on the rib under the tailpin gut. He frequently used open grained wood for the tables, and a red/brown varnish.

THORN W.G. *Southampton*
c. 1935 Quite nice work on the Stradivarius pattern.

THORN William c. 1875 *South Molton*

THOROWGOOD Henry c. 1760 *London*

THORBURN S.W. *Symington Mill*
Worked c. 1912 and inscribed his name on the inner back. Average work using wood of small figure and varnished a deep red.

THOUVENOT E.M. c.1910   *London*

THOW John   *Dundee*
Worked c. 1870 using Stradivarius and Guarnerius models but enalarging them,
his work is good and he used nicely figured wood. The varnish is an oil
preparation in shades of golden brown. They are stamped THOW/DUNDEE
below the button.

TILLER C.W.   *Boscombe & Bournemouth*
A cabinet maker who made some excellent instruments, one such dated 1920
on a Stradivarius model using a well figured two piece back, strongly grained
table wood and varnished a deep brown.

TILLER Wilfred b1917   *Martock*
A carpenter who started making violins as a result of having read E.H. Varney's
series of articles on violin making in 'Woodworker'. First instruments made
about 1958. His work is excellent and his output numbered about 50 violins,
10 violas and 1 'cello.

TILLEY Thomas   *London*
Worked c. 1770 - 1790 with neat workmanship. Rather small model and fairly
highly arched. His 'cellos are 750mm in body length, the model very rounded
top and bottom, nicely figured woods and varnished orange/brown. Label in
M/S Thomas "Tilley/from Market Lane, St. James, London, 1786".

TINNEY A.E.   *Bristol*
I do not know whether he made any instruments under his own name. He
worked for Geo. Darbey and then took over his shop and worked there until a
great age as a repairer and dealer.

TIPPER J.W.   *Derby*
Probably an amateur maker. His violins are attractive and well made. Worked c.
1918.

TIVEY J.H.   *Quorn*
Worked c. 1970.

TOBIN James   *London*
Son of Richard and his work is very similar. Period 1830 - 1850.

TOBIN Richard   *London*
He worked initially with Thos. Perry in Dublin and came to London about 1798 to
work for John Betts and others until he opened a small shop in Shug Lane.
Frequently his work is unlabelled but sometimes branded TOBIN below the button.
That which is labelled proves him to be a good workman but so many anonymous
instruments are ascribed to him on scanty evidence that his whole work and
productivity is rather a mystery: many of these 'ascribed to' instruments are pretty
ordinary affairs. One characteristic of his violins is that, like Perry, the stop is often
short. On the best work the varnish is good, very often a plum red/brown in shade.

TODD G.   *Tweedmouth, Berwick*
Worked c. 1900.

TOLLEY William Henry b1894   *Miles Platting*
Amateur. Pattern maker by trade. He worked c. 1924.

TOLMIE G.   *Hanwell*
Amateur working c. 1900 - 1920. Good workmanship and choice of woods. No.
18 - a 16" viola with one piece back and nicely made - was dated 1914.

TOMALIN N.   *Gussage All Saints*
A self taught amateur of only average ability c. 1960.

TOOMEY Timothy b1868 d1954   *Bolsover, Fulham & Enfield*
Violonist and teacher. He made a fair number of violins, violas and 'cellos of
above average amateur ability, good choice of wood and no fault to find with
the workmanship. He made an oil varnish which was very satifactory and
which he marketed along with 'Toomey' resin. Label· "No. 18 Made by
1923/Timothy Toomey/London England". 'Cellos rather on the heavy side, a
fault which applies to many English 'cellos of this period.

TOPHAM Carass   *Abingdon*
Amateur c. 1960-1980.

TORR Ernest b1871   *Liverpool*
Initially self taught from books, later worked for G. Byrom. He made his first
instruments in 1903. The violins are on conventional models and very
satisfactory tonally. Also made several violas and 'cellos.

TRANTOR Thomas   *Liverpool*
Probably an amateur maker working c. 1900 from the evidence of two violins
bearing his name. His work was above average and nicely varnished a deep red.

TRINGHAM Henry c.1850   *Shrewsbury*

TROTMAN William H.   *Hereford*
Worked c. 1850.

TRUEMAN Richard   *Bath*
Worked c. 1825 on the Amati model to produce a few nice violins.

TUBBS Alfred d1911   *London*
Bowmaker. Son of James.

TUBBS Edward 1832 - 1922   *London, later New York*
Bowmaker.

TUBBS James 1835 - 1921   *London*
Son of William and the most famous English bowmaker. Early work when
employed by W.E. Hill stamped W.E. HILL (sometimes this stamp is obliterated by
Tubbs own stamp applied later). His bows are stamped "Jas. TUBBS", they are
functional pieces of work rather than having great beauty. The ferrule is long and
rounded at the end, the heads have a small chamfer and no ridge to the front of the
head, the face (always metal apart from the bows made for Hill) is abruptly turned
up at the peak so that the metal stands above the wood, sticks almost invariably

round and dark (sometimes so dark as to be almost black), adjusters always silver or gold on ebony. Some violin bows very light and whippy (very often these sticks are nearly black), 'cello bows weighty. Frogs sometimes plain sometimes with a pearl eye, the eyes never ringed. Many copies of his bows exist duly stamped as such, and some are very deceptive because they may be fine bows.

TUBBS William 1814 - 1878   *London*
Father of James. He was first employed by Dodd and set up his own shop later. He made bows which are stamped with his name and many for dealers which are stamped with their names.

TUBBS Thomas   *London*
Father of William. His bows are copies of Dodd and very good.

TURNBULL William   *Dundee*
c. 1870. An amateur maker who worked circa 1870 - 1890 and made a number of instruments of reasonably good workmanship on a slightly large Guarnerius pattern. Label "W. Turnbull/Maker/Dundee 1878".

TURNER John Alvey 1790 - 1862   *London*
Instruments labelled or stamped 'TURNER' (under the button or lengthways under the tailpiece) were not made by him but by workmen in his employ, or imported from the continent principally from Mittenwald. Some of these, particularly 'cellos, are good.

TWEEDALE Charles L.   *Weston, Wharfdale*
Vicar of Weston who, between 1900 and 1940 made a large quantity of violins allegedly assisted by spiritualism. His instruments are based principally on Stradivarius and Guarnerius models but are frequently larger, some as long in the body as 362mm. The workmanship is satisfactory and they are quite well varnished. Many of them are given names e.g. Lamorak (1911), Maureen (1913), Rowena (1909).

TWEMLOW S.P. c. 1925   *Sandbach*

TYE J.   *London*
Worked c. 1850 quite neat work. Label "Made by J. Tye/37 Agnes Street, York Road/Lambeth, London.

TYSON Herbert William 1878 - circa 1959   *Louth*
A wheelwright who made a good number of violins, violas, 'cellos and at least one double bass. His work, on standard patterns, is heavy but in no way crude. He used a good oil varnish generally golden brown shades. The double bass was well made on the Panormo model with a whole back and the belly made of Pirana pine cut on the slab and varnished with a brown, probably spirit, varnish.

URQUHART Alexander   *Invergordon*
Probably an amateur. He made a number of violins c. 1920 on a large Stradivarius pattern. His name is written on the bare wood inside the back "Alex. Urquhart/Invergordon".

URQUHART David b1859   *Dundee*

URQUHART Donald   *Tain (N.B.)*
Amateur maker but his work is much above average on a large Stadivarius pattern and varnished with a fine oil varnish made by himself. M/S label "Donald Urquhart/Tain N.B. 18–".

URQUHART Thomas   *London*
Worked from about 1650 - 1680. His violins are generally highly arched and not very elegant but some are smaller with the arching less: his instruments have a small but very clear tone. The varnish an oil one, is particularly good.

VALENTINE William   *London*
Worked circa 1870, specialising in double bass making.

VAN DER GEEST b1899   *London & Johannesburg*
He worked for Hart & Son until he left for Johannesburg in 1938 and while with Hart made some of the violins bearing their label.

VARNEY E.H.   *London*
Worked for E & P Voigt c. 1950: perhaps best known for a series of articles which he wrote for the 'Woodworker' on Violin Making. I have not seen any of his work.

VAUGHAN b1860   *Chester*
Worked as an amateur maker of no little merit c. 1925.

VAUGHAN J.   *Dublin*
Worked c. 1880, his work is reasonably good.

VAUS W.   *Hackney/London*
Worked c. 1925.

VERNON John Maurice 1901 - 1970   *London*
A good amateur maker, pupil and close friend of Geo. Wulme-Hudson.

VICTOR T.   *London*
The pseudonym of Victor Thomassin. He worked in London as a bow-maker during the first quarter of the 20th century and used the stamp T. VICTOR to avoid confusion with other members of the family. He worked a good deal for the trade.

VINCENT Alfred 1877 - 1947   *London & Brighton*
A professional violinist who started violin making as a hobby and adopted it as a professional maker very successfully. His output was over 300 instruments of very fine workmanship. The violins are on the pattern of Stradivarius and sometimes just a shade on the small side. The workmanship and selection of wood is excellent. He was assisted by his brother and some instruments are labelled "A & H Vincent/40 Grafton Sq., Soho".

VINOT Louis Thomas   *London*
Known only as a splendid violin Stradivarius copy, orange brown varnish labelled "Copy of Strad/Louis Th. Vinot Maker 1897/18 East St., Bldgs, Manchester Sq., London".

VLUMMENS D.C. b1885 *London*
Pupil of his father Isidor. After working for several firms in London he started in business for himself in 1925. His violins are very well made on Stradivarius and Guarnerius models.

VOIGT Arnold 1864 - 1952 *London, later Markneukirchen*
He worked in City Rd. London for five years 1885 - 1890. During this time he made numerous instruments and these are personal work, later, in Markneukirchen, most of those bearing his name are of the workshop variety.

VOIGT Paul Arne 1881 - 1970 *Manchester*
Apprenticed to E.R. Schmidt and later worked for Richard Weichold. He came to England in 1905 and worked for some time for Thos. Hesketh before setting up in business on his own account at 37 Plymouth Avenue, Manchester. He made numerous instruments of first class workmanship some of which are oversize. On some of his instruments the varnish has badly crazed.

VOIGT Paul 1912 - 1992 *London & Northwood*
Son of Paul Arne, apprenticed in Markneukirchen for 4 years and returned to help his father for a short while before joining brother Ernest in Shaftesbury Avenue. After 5 years in the services he returned and joined Ernest in business as E & P Voigt, Monmouth St., later in 1955 he left to work on his own in Gerrard Place. Many of the E & P Voigt instruments were made by him. He was renowned as a restorer and expert connoisseur.

VOLLER William, Charles & Arthur *London*
Always grouped together as Voller Bros they worked c. 1885 - 1925. Their instruments are remarkably good imitations of classical Italian instruments, the ageing being most skilfully done with no exaggerations of style or wear. One of them was the maker of the infamous 'Balfour' Strad.

VOYLE Benjamin *Swansea*
c. 1860. Average class of work.

VRINT Peter (II) *London*
He worked in Charing Cross Road. His violins are of rather large build. Instead of a label he often wrote the details on the inner back and branded his name below the button. Certainly working up to 1910.

VRINT C. *London*
Brother of the above and associated with G. Pryce, London.

WADE Joseph *Leeds*
He made well over 100 instruments all carefully made and well varnished, a feature of the scrolls is the splendid undercutting gradually deepening to become very deep at the eye. Printed label. "Joseph Wade/Armley/Leeds 1889".

WADE William 19th century *Leeds*

WALKER F.P. c. 1930 *Sunderland*

WALKER Hector M. c. 1925 *Liverpool*
20th century, his work is said to be good.

WALKER J. *London*
Worked at 370 Kennington Road, principally a repairer.

WALKER Henry *Stoke on Trent*
Working c. 1910, amateur maker, good work mainly violins but some violas and one 'cello known.

WALKER Henry J. *Whitby*
Amateur maker who used the Stradivarius pattern to produce some well made violins and violas during the period 1890 - 1905. The violins are made on a Stradivarius model and the violas are a useful size at 415mm body length.

WALKER John 1876 - 1958 *Birmingham*
Being so much in demand as a repairer prevented J. Walker from making more than about 50 instruments but these are fine examples of craftmanship; he also made some violas. Label "John Walker/Solihull, Birmingham/Fecit anno 1950", sometimes he branded his name on the centre bout linings.

WALKER John c. 1840 *Martley, Worcestershire*

WALKER R. *Hawick*
Worked c. 1890 making some fine instruments in the Stradivarius pattern.

WALKER William b1859 *Mid Calder & Broxburn*
Amateur maker whose output was over 150 instruments of excellent workmanship and style during the period circa 1890 - 1925. The varnish is an oil one golden brown and orange brown being the favoured shades. Label "William Walker Fecit/Broxburn Anno 1922".

WALL Robert Frederick b1882 *London & Jersey*
Amateur maker who made only a few instruments.

WALLACE Alfred c. 1900 *Guernsey*

WALLACE P. *Berwick*
Probably an amateur maker, very neat work on an over long model with ink lines substituting for purfling. Good materials and varnished a nice golden brown.

WALMSLEY Arthur c. 1914 *Burnley & Blackpool*

WALTON F.L. C.1920 *Hanley*

WALTON R. c.1918 *Hanley*

WALTON William b1860 *Longton, Preston*
Initially an amateur maker who later turned professional. Probably self taught and his first instrument dated 1887. For his violins the model is a personal one having bits of the classical makers eclectically combined, workmanship very sound using good materials the whole covered with an oil varnish generally shades of golden brown. Working period c1887 - 1930. He also made some bows but these are unstamped. Label "William Walton/Maker/Longton, Preston/A.D. 1928 No. 74".

WAMSLEY Peter *London*

Worked c. 1715 - 1750 chiefly on the Stainer pattern for violins but occasionally on a less highly arched model. His violins are not highly regarded despite the fact that they are frequently very attractive with nicely figured backs and a reddish brown varnish. Some are less good and often these are without purfling. His 'cellos are more highly regarded and he made a lot of them, they are very rounded top and bottom, of around 735mm body length, generally using handsome wood for the backs, seldom purfled and having a very flat part to the table under the bridge. This portion is left too thick and the response is killed. He also made some double basses which are well thought of.

WARD c1830 *Warrington*

WARD George *Dublin*

Worked circa 1710 - 1768. His instruments are very good using handsome wood and a fine varnish. The purfling is often omitted and ink lines substituted.

WARD Robert *Liverpool*

Worked c. 1935 making violins and violas. His instruments are quite well made and are both labelled and branded on the back.

WARDE William c. 1860 *London*

WARDLAW Richard *Cardiff*

c. 1900 Amateur. Average merit.

WAREHAM H.F. *London*

Working c. 1920. Maker of the 'Patonzi-Cremona violins.

WARRICK Albert E. b1863 *Leeds*

Pupil of G.A. Chanot. Fine work on chiefly Guarnerius but also Stradivarius models, good materials and covered with a fine varnish the ruby red shade being particularly attractive.

WARRICK A. *Portchester, Portsmouth*

Working period 1930-1950. His instruments are well made but often suffer from the defect that has beset many British makers, namely unstable varnish. So far as is known he had no relationship to the other entries having the same name.

WARRICK Alfred 1890 - 1962 *Leeds & London*

Son and pupil of the Albert E.. Worked with his father until 1923 when he went to work for Dykes and later on his own in Eccleston Road, Ealing.

WARRICK Reginald *Northampton*

c. 1890. Amateur maker.

WATERFIELD J.D.   *Nottingham*
20th century, violin maker, repairer and dealer.

WATSON Francis B. c.1928   *Sheffield*

WATSON Frank b1866   *Rochdale*
Pupil of Priestnall and made about 200 excellent instruments. The violins are
on an original model, a varient of Stradivarius, and many are over long in the
body, 365mm is quite common. Printed label "Frank Watson/Maker/Rochdale,
Lancashire/No. 31 — 1900". Varnish shades of red, red/brown or deep orange.
Also made a few bows.

WATSON John   *Lerwick*
A priest at Lerwick who made about 50 violins neatly but frequently on a very
eccentric pattern.

WATSON John D. c. 1920   *Belfast*

WATSON Thomas Kay b1883   *Edinburgh*
Worked in Edinburgh from about 1927 to 1948 as an amateur but the
workmanship is worthy of a professional maker. The backs are often very
handsomely figured, the fronts are generally quite broad grained. The varnish is
an oil one and occasionally unstable.

WATT Alexander Stocks 1859 - 1908   *Edinburgh*
Amateur maker pupil of Dr. G. Dickson. Violins generally in the style of
Guarnerius. Made about 50 violins and a few violas. Label "Mr. Alex S.
Watt/Made in ye olde Burgh of Inverkeithing A.D. 1895".

WATT Walter 1787 - 1826   *Glasgow*

WATT Walter   *High Blantyre*
Working c. 1885.

WATT William Reid 1885   *Birmingham*
A pupil of Frank Howard after having made a few violins self taught. Very good
choice of materials and satisfactory, if not good, workmanship. Varnish
generally a dark red.

WATTS R.   *London*
Period c. 1790. It is probable that instruments bearing the name of "R. Watts
Musical Warehouse" were made for him by others.

WAYLETT Henry   *London*
Worked c. 1765 in Exeter Exchange, The Strand. Fairly highly arched violins
and violas with deep ribs.

WEAVER Samuel   *London*
Indifferent work c. 1790

WEBSTER Andrew c. 1867   *Leith*

WEBB George *Bristol*
Worked in Lower Park Row as a maker, repairer and dealer between the wars.

WEBB William c. 1924 *London*

WEBB Robert J. 1914 - 1950 *London*
Made some splendid violins on the Stradivarius model; also a few Tertis model violas. Varnish red/brown and golden/brown.

WEBBER C. *Coulsdon*
Worked c. 1954 - 1960 in a small shop in High Rd., Coulsdon. He made a good number of violins swiftly but the workmanship is indifferent, they are varnished with a yellowish shade of spirit varnish, some of them sounded quite pleasing.

WEBSTER Andrew *Leith*
Worked c. 1870 possibly a repairer only.

WEBSTER George died c. 1983 *Aberdeen*
Worked between about 1945 - 1975. His work is rather variable but none of it reaching a high standard. The violins are on a large Stradivarius model often as long as 364mm. The backs are generally plain but occasionally he used well figured wood. Varnish a dull yellow brown shade.

WEBSTER Patrick *Leeds*
Contemporary.

WEBSTER Richard *Bathgate*
Worked c. 1918 and made some nice violins from well figured wood; some double purfled. Golden orange varnish.

WELLBY Charles b1863 *Edinburgh*
He made a number of excellent violins using classical models and varnishing them in shades of red. He worked from about 1888 to 1930, probably an amateur since his early work is by no means so good as that from, say 1900 onwards.

WELCH J.S. c. 1890 *Manchester*

WELLER Frederick *Holmwood, Surrey*
Violinist who was self taught as a maker, became a professional and made upwards of 250 good instruments mainly violins. Label in M/S "Fredk. W: Weller/Holmwood/Surrey/No. 81-1947".

WHEATLEY John *Dublin*
Worked c. 1825 in Abbey St., later in partnership with Ringwood.

WHITAKER John *London*
Worked c. 1820 and for some time in partnership with Button. His instruments fall into the second class trade type generally of plain wood and unpurfled. Some of the 'cellos are better, these are made from figured wood, purfled and of quite good workmanship. Label "Made & sold by John Whitaker & Co./75 St. Paul's Churchyard, London 1824".

WHITBREAD William Walter b1974 *Southsea*
An amateur whose instruments are rather too substantially built, some of rather eccentric design too.

WHITELAW James *Glasgow*
Not a maker but included here since his varnish is so often referred to. This he produced at 496 St. George's Rd., Glasgow being "A genuine and beautiful oil varnish made from fossil gum amber". It was sold in a packet of two bottles together with surfacing and polishing powder for 7/6 (37½p) in 1880. It certainly was an improvement on many varnishes previously used but was very prone to chip.

WHITE Ernest E. b1887 *Wednesfield*
Amateur. Stradivarius style, name etc written inside the back.

WHITE Henry J. *Ealing & London*
Professional violinist who turned to violin making full time having made some as a hobby. Worked at Ealing in 1924 later in Frith St., London.

WHITE James *Edinburgh*
Worked c. 1870, very satisfactory work.

WHITE John *Camerton*
Made violins and 'cellos.

WHITE John c. 1910 *Barnard Castle*

WHITE T.S. c. 1970 *Market Harborough*

WHITE Wilfred *Pudsey*
c. 1950 - 1980. Amateur maker.

WHITEHEAD Gerald *Southport*
c. 1925 Amateur maker.

WHITEHEAD L. *London*
Probably an amateur maker. No. 21 dated 1887 showed fair workmanship.

WHITESIDE Henry 1746 - 1824 *Liverpool & Solva*
Made some violins as an amateur in Liverpool then moved to Pembrokeshire to build the lighthouse at Solva. While doing so he continued to make instruments and these are of average merit, several have the backs and ribs made from beech wood.

WHITMARSH Emmanuel *London*
A self taught violin maker who was originally a stonemason. He moved around London between 1856 and 1908 when he settled at Dalston. A prolific maker who made not only under his own name but also for dealers for whom he repaired instruments. His work, despite the cheap prices for which he sold it, is excellent. In violins his Guarnerius style instruments are good and of correct size using handsome wood and varnished well. He also made violas and 'cellos. His instruments are mostly labelled in manuscript but later he used a printed label: often they are unlabelled and his name will be found written in an obscure place inside the back in pencil with the date. A much under rated maker.

WHITMARSH Edwin   *London*
Son of the above and worked certainly until 1942. In no way is his work so good as his father's.

WILD Frank b.1869   *Rochdale*
An amateur maker who made a number of excellent violins on the Stradivarius model.

WIGAN David   *Shrewsbury*
An amateur maker of no small ability who worked c. 1900.

WIGHTMAN George   *London*
Label "George Wightman/Wood Street, London 1761".

WILKIN G.H.   *Hull*
An amateur maker c. 1910 whose work is pretty feeble.

WILKINSON J.T. b1870
Amateur maker.

WILKINSON R. c. 1970   *Derby*

WILKINSON Samuel Blakeley 1853 - 1895   *Leeds*
Professional maker who made about 30 violins of rather variable workmanship the best of which are generally varnished with a deep red varnish. While the workmanship on the best is good, the appearance is amateurish due to thick raised edges wide and deeply scooped corners etc.

WILKINSON John 1889 - 1961   *London*
A professional maker who never labelled his instruments. He worked mainly for the trade making principally violins on the Guarnerius model with grafted necks and other subterfuges to make them look old. The materials not always of the best indeed it is very often quite plain, the backs slab cut, and the outline sometimes not symmetrical about the centre line. The violas are large, 422mm is a common size, often with plain slab backs, the outline having a nasty stiff 'C' and heavily built. Notwithstanding all the obvious imperfections they are solidly made - indeed often weighty-and highly regarded. It is said that he never made a 'cello, but the author had one signed inside the belly and dated 1920 of good wood and varnished red.

WILKS Alfred c. 1900   *Manchester*

WILKS David c. 1910   *Manchester*

WILLIAMS Alfred b1840   *Cheltenham*
Worked at 8 Gt. Western Road as a professional maker and produced some good instruments.

WILLIAMS Arthur b1877   *Barnes*
Pupil of Frank Howard. Really excellent violins in the style of Guarnerius using the best of materials and a fine orange brown varnish. Work of truly professional quality. Label "A. Williams/1938 London".

WILLIAMS Benjamin 1768 - 1839   *Aberavon*
Made about 80 violins on an Amati model using, it is said, local timber. His varnishing method was to rub linseed oil and turpentine into the bare wood and then apply four coats of spirit varnish.

WILLIAMS O.R. 1910   *Manchester*

WILLIAMS R.J. b.1865   *Llandudno*
A self taught amateur and a very clever maker who subsequently became a professional. Made violins, violas and 'cellos. In all he made about 60 instruments.

WILLIAMS Robert R.   *Porth, Rhondda*
c. 1920 Rather large Stradivarius outline.

WILLIAMS Robert Stephen b.1892   *Liverpool*
A pupil of R.H. Bird and worked for Rushworth & Dreaper making some of the 'Ardeton' instruments (q.v.).

WILLIAMS Thomas b.1864   *Edgbaston*
Amateur maker but his work is of a high quality.

WILLIAMSON Thomas Aguste   *Cambuslang*
Worked c. 1890. His work is neatly finished on a rather narrow model with high arching and straight set soundholes. Varnish a dark brown probably spirit based. The tone was inclined to be shrill. Label "Thomas Aguste Williamson/ Cambuslang 1894".

WILLIS A.   *London*
Bowmaker who worked for Hill's and left them in 1966.

WILLIS Charles Silk b1883   *Reading*
An amateur maker who had some instruction from Chanot in London. He made few instruments but he carried out a large number of repairs and was active as a dealer. Label "C.S. Willis/Maker/Reading 19..".

WILLMORE Josiah J. b1877   *Wood Green, London*
Pupil of Frank Howard. An amateur maker who made few well constructed instruments circa 1925.

WILSON Frederick   *Chelmsford*
Worked c. 1910 - 1925. Probably an amateur maker, his work is of good quality. No. 19 dated 1921.

WILSON J. Gorden   *Glasgow*
Worked c. 1880. Amateur. Very fair workmanship but the whole conception is too heavy.

WILSON James   *Belkington*
Worked c. 1880 and made a number of violins on the 'long Strad' model.

WILSON James   *Mauchline*
Worked c. 1920. Probably an amateur whose work is of above average merit.

WILSON J.J.T. *London*
Bowmaker and violin repairer. Pupil of Jas, Tubbs for bows and later worked for Chas Boullangier. Established on his own in 1882 in Percy Street where he was certainly working in 1930. Bows stamped J.J.T. WILSON or sometimes just WILSON.

WILSON James L. b.1847 *Greenock*
Pupil of Mann and worked on conventional classical models with great success using Whitelaw's varnish generally red in colour. He made relatively few instruments and these are signed with his name inside the back, sometimes with the number and date (No. 16 - 1898).

WILSON Joseph b.1880 *Glasgow & Edinburgh*
A dentist who made a large number of violins of good workmanship.

WILTON James *Whitby*
Worked for H.J. Walker of Whitby and later on his own. Good average work.

WILSON Thomas c. 1948 *Grimsby*

WILSON William *Clydebank*
Amateur maker working circa 1927.

WINFIELD F.E. *Derby*
Pupil of A.J. Roberts. First instrument made in 1921. His violins are modelled after Stradivarius and Guarnerius and are well made.

WINTER & SON c. 1880 *Hull*

WISE Christopher *London*
Worked c. 1660. The outline of his instruments is curious since the top width is not much less than that of the bottom, body length short. Arching medium high and deep ribs. Short corner projection. Worked in Half Moon Alley and later Vine Court.

WITHERS Edward I 1808 - 1875 *London*
He bought Davis's business in Coventry Street and had several fine makers e.g. J.F. Lott, Maucotel, Boullangier working for him. His own work is very good and frequently covered with a rich deep red varnish.

WITHERS Edward II 1844 - 1915 *London*
Son and pupil of the above and worked for 24 years with his father. Very productive maker using Stradivarius and Guarnerius models and his instruments reach a high standard. Also made violas and 'cellos. Inventor of the 'Withers hollow soundpost' and a 'Tubular bass bar'; innovations which have little merit.

WITHERS George 1847 - 1931 *London*
Son of Edward I. Trained at Mirecourt. Many instruments are labelled as from George Withers or Geo. Withers & Sons but it is not possible to identify which were personally made and which were made by their many workman. Many of those labelled "oil varnished etc." were imported from France in the white and some are capital instruments.

WITHERS Joseph 1838 died after 1920 *London*
Worked for James Brown of Spitalfields having commenced to make violins as a hobby in 1856. Later worked on his own account from 156 Caledonian Rd. N. London. Violins are on the pattern of the Messie Strad. He also made violas (generally rather on the small side) - and 'cellos. His output was about 150 violins, 12 violas and a few 'cellos.

WOLLEN F. J. *Barnstaple*
Probably an amateur maker. M/S lable "F. J. Wollen/18 Maker 87/ Barnstaple N. Devon". Quite good work.

WOOD George *London*
Known only by a nicely made violin 358mm body length well figured back and ribs, Amati-Strad style, long corners, edges nicely raised, button rather squat, other details nicely handled, golden varnish. The tone was not great however, the belly being 5mm thick at the centre tapering to 2.5mm at the edges. No label but signed inside the back "George Wood fecit/London 1830".

WOOD George *Liverpool*
Worked circa 1880-1905. His work is on the Stradivarius model and carefully finished with a good oil varnish generally orange/brown in colour. Label "Made by Geo Wood/Liverpool 1899. No. 38"

WOOD James b.1884 *Perth*
Cabinet maker who made some quite good violins. Label "James Wood" No. 8 Perth 1927".

WOOD J *Bradford*
Worked as an amateur maker c 1913 using Guarnerius as a model. His work is of fair quality and varnished golden brown.

WOODWARD C. F. *Kettering*
Commenced making as an amateur in 1946. His output is not large and besides violins includes violas (some on the Tertis model) and 'cellos. He used locally grown woods and an oil varnish.

WOOLLEN A. H. b. 1923 *Whetstone*
Amateur maker and pupil of Raymond Franks. An industrial chemist by profession. He made 13 violins, some small size, and a few guitars all very neatly.

WOODWARD – *Birmingham*
Worked c 1830 using good materials. The pattern is akin to that of Jacob Stainer with reduced arching. No label but branded WOODWARD in small capitals on the back.

WORDEN James b 1839 d 1910 *Preston*
Worked at 83 Friargate. Originally a cabinet maker and organ builder who turned to violin making and repairing as a trade. His violins are suggestive of Stradivarius but they are over long in the body (363mm is quite common). The work is good. Label "Jacobus Worden/Prestonensis/Faciebat Anno 1904/Sub titulo Sancte Joachim".

WORKMAN James   *Kilmarnock*
Worked circa 1880.

WORTHINGTON John   *Hereford*
Worked c 1820, highly built indifferently made violins.

WORTHY W. H.   *Helmsley*
His work is said to be good. Worked c 1950

WREDE H.   *London*
c 1820. His name is listed in some directories but his work seems to have vanished.

WRIGHT A.   *Southampton*
Amateur maker c 1920. His work is not good

WRIGHT Daniel   *London*
c 1740. Label "Made by Daniel Wright/in Holborn, London".

WRIGHT Ebenezer   *South Shields*
c 1880. Fairly poor quality of work.

WRIGHT Haydn W.   *Brockley & Brixton*
Worked c 1925. He was a pupil of Frank Howard.

WRIGHT J.   *Slough*
Cobbler by trade. Worked c 1925 and made a few carefully worked violins.

WRIGHT Joseph   *Derby*
c 1890. Instruments bearing his label were bought by him 'in the white'. Varnished and 'decorated' by him.

WROZINA Ignaz   *Edinburgh*
Worked for Methven & Simpson c 1885 and later on his own. His instruments, violins, violas and 'cellos are carefully made and well finished.

WRYATT Angus   *Portobello*
C 1710 Rough work with fanciful carvings instead of normal scrolls.

WYMERS John   *Cambridge*
Worked mid 18th century. From the evidence of a 'cello of 732mm body length made from well figured woods, very rounded outline top and bottom and neatly purfled, his work must have been very good.

YATES A.   *Stockport*
As an amateur made about 20 instruments circa 1890 1910. Average work.

YATES Henry   *Streatham*
Worked at 17 Pendennis Road during the early part of the 20th century, his work is said to be very good.

YATES Richard b 1863   *Manchester*
Pattern maker and amateur violin maker from 1884. He made few instruments and the early ones were not so good; later example are good both in workmanship and tone.

YEOMAN Sydney B.   *London*
Bowmaker with Hill's throughout his working life.

YOOLE William b.1806 d.1868   *St. Andrews*
Pupil of Matthew Hardie and later Thomas Hardie. He made few instruments some of them with Thos. Hardie's assistance. It is recorded that his production was 8 violins, 1 viola and 2 'cellos and these are of good workmanship.

YOUNG George R. b.1875 d.1936   *Colchester*
Amateur maker self taught who made a number of excellent violins and violas. His instruments are dated from Vevey, New York and Colchester.

YOUNG Harry   *Islington*
Made a few instruments c 1960 but was mainly occupied with repairs.

YOUNG James c 1890   *Edinburgh*

YOUNG John b 1812 d 1866   *Aberdeen*
Not very careful work and the woods not always very good but the tone of his instruments is generally all right. Made violins, violas and 'cellos. Label "J. Young/Maker, Aberdeen" and often stamped YOUNG/Abdn.

YOUNG Thomas D   *Rutherglen*
Probably an amateur maker. He worked c 1914 and from the evidence of a violin on the Stradivarius model was capable of good work.

YOUNGMAN Marshall 1860-1924   *Halifax*
Initally an amateur maker who decided to become a professional in 1890. He made 48 violins, 6 violas and 6 'cellos. The workmanship is good although the instruments are rather heavily built especially the 'cellos. Label "M. Youngman/ Halifax/No. 38 A.D. 1921".

YOUNGSON Alexander   *Glasgow*
Worked c 1970 and made some quite good violins and violas (on the Tertis model). The style is inclined to be heavy with sharply raised edges. No. 33 dated 1974.

ZETTWITZ William   *Liverpool, Auckland, London.*
First rate maker who made violins, violas and 'cellos. Established at King St. Hammersmith under the name Zettwitz & Son. Branded WZ below the button and sometimes Wm. Zettwitz inside the back.